Why Don't Jews Believe in Jesus
A Jewish-Christian Unfolds the Great Mystery

Eitan Bar

Copyright © 2023 Eitan Bar
All rights reserved.
ISBN: 9798850839383

Please, quote freely from this book only if including the author and book's names with a link to the book's Amazon page.

All scripture quotations, unless otherwise indicated, are taken from The Holy Bible, New International Version®, NIV®. Copyright © 1973, 1978, 1984, 2011 by Biblica, Inc.® Used by permission of Zondervan. All rights reserved worldwide. The "NIV" and "New International Version" are trademarks registered in the United States Patent and Trademark Office by Biblica, Inc.® Scripture quotations marked ESV are taken from the ESV® Bible (The Holy Bible, English Standard Version®). Copyright © 2001 by Crossway, a publishing ministry of Good News Publishers. Used by permission. All rights reserved.

IN DEDICATION TO THE JEWISH PEOPLE

*For I bear them witness that they have a zeal
for God, but not according to knowledge.
(Romans 10:2)*

CONTENTS

Preface vi

Introduction viii

Reason #1:
THE LIES WE TELL OURSELVES 20

    Israel's Religion 21

    Rabbinic Judaism vs. Christian Judaism 37

    Jewish Theological Objections to Jesus 45

Reason #2:
WHAT WAS DONE TO US IN JESUS'S NAME 59

    Replacement Theology 60

    Antisemitism 77

    The Holocaust 106

    Modern-day Antisemitism 116

Reason #3:
WHAT CHRISTIANS TELL US ABOUT OUR GOD 129

    Christian Misuse of the Torah in Evangelism 135

    The Gospel Presentation Jews Can't Embrace 142

Epilogue 183

Endnotes 186

PREFACE

In December of 2022, days before the glow of Christmas, I found myself driving toward Nazareth for a musical performance of "Elijah." The act was a grand collaboration between Jewish, Arab, and German artists, hosted within the grandeur of the Maronite Church in Nazareth. My ride was a modest 2010 Seat Ibiza, a small car that had seen better days. As I journeyed uphill, my old vehicle strained against the slope, eventually crying out with alarming beeps before breaking down right as I reached my final destination.

In this moment of dread, a good Samaritan showed up out of the blue—an Arab Maronite—belonging to the Eastern Catholic denomination. He assessed my car with a practiced eye, and as it happened, he had just what was needed in his car to fix mine! We set to work and soon had my little Ibiza purring again. Despite my insistence, the angel refused to accept any compensation for his aid.

In the course of our interaction, I disclosed to him that I was a Jewish believer in Jesus. He paused, gave me a long look, and remarked, "Wow, I've heard about your kind, but I've never met one before!" His words made me feel somewhat special, yet they underscored the fact that Jews typically don't believe in Jesus.

Finally, inside the expansive church, the performance began. The orchestra harmonized beautifully, breathing life into the story of "Elijah." The narrative, however, was poignant - it spoke of Israel straying from God and seeking other deities while God endlessly endeavored to win them back. A feeling of melancholy swept over me as I sat among hundreds of my fellow Jews, most of them likely secular. As far as I knew, I was the only Jewish believer in Jesus there, a sobering realization that added a note of loneliness to an otherwise captivating evening.

A couple of points before we begin.

1. Translations of quotes from Hebrew to English have been carried out by me. In a few exceptional cases, translations were made from an English text that had already been translated into Hebrew, essentially translating a translation back to English. This approach was taken when the original English text was inaccessible to me.

2. The footnotes in this book are meant to enrich your reading experience further, don't skip them. However, for a smoother reading experience, footnotes that are plain references to sources (like books, articles, videos, or URLs) were converted to endnotes and are available at the very end of the book.

Therefore, subscripts of Roman numerals (IX, XXII, etc.) are the footnotes you should care about (and in the print version, will be available at the bottom of the page), while subscripts numbering 1-300 are endnotes that were moved to the end of the book (and you can feel free to ignore them).

INTRODUCTION

I am one of fewer than five thousand Israeli-born adult Jewish believers in Jesus in Israel.[1] I have also spent the last two decades engaged in profound and, at times, intense discussions with my fellow Jews regarding the messiahship of Jesus, whom I acknowledge as my own Jewish Messiah. My journey has led me to explore countless books, videos, and articles in both Hebrew and English that explore the Jewish objections to Jesus. I have participated in numerous conversations with Jewish people about the gospel, some lasting for months. During the past twenty years, I have witnessed many Jews of various backgrounds, from secular to orthodox, embracing Jesus Christ in remarkable ways. Most of them, however, ended up leaving our messianic movement.

In what was a ground-breaking event for me, I became the first Jewish follower of Jesus to debate with an Orthodox Jewish rabbi and Rosh Kollel (head of a seminary) in the Hebrew language in the Land of Israel. This has never happened before.

In the summer of 2022, just a few weeks before I left ONE FOR ISRAEL Ministry,[II] a prominent rabbi told one of my co-workers, "*Eitan Bar is the greatest threat to Orthodox Judaism since Paul the Apostle.*" Although this statement was meant as a criticism, and later you will understand why, I took it as a tremendous compliment. I mention this not to boast but to highlight my unique position. Firstly, I am a

---

[1] We'll discuss Jewish believers in Israel in greater detail later in the book.
[II] To learn about the circumstances of my leaving, see: www.eitan.bar/oneforisrael

Jesus-following Jew born and raised in Israel, the homeland of the Jewish people, as well as of Jesus and his disciples. Secondly, I have spent nearly twenty years sharing Christ with my Jewish brothers and sisters. I have engaged in thousands of conversations, including debates with rabbis and an atheist Jewish Bible professor.

Moreover, I have dedicated most of my life to the study of the Bible and theology, earning my bachelor's, master's, and doctorate degrees in the process. This journey has provided me with substantial insight and the ability to explain why Jews don't believe in Jesus. Over the past few years, I have lectured worldwide on why Jews reject Christianity. Once, I uploaded my lecture to YouTube, allowing friends who couldn't attend the conference where I spoke to watch it. To my surprise, the lecture garnered five million views; I had no idea so many people were interested in the subject!

This book is the culmination of my thoughts, research, and personal experiences, woven together to provide a comprehensive analysis answering one of the most complex questions there is: "Why don't Jews believe in Jesus?"

Undoubtedly, the reasons behind Jewish nonbelief in Jesus are multifaceted and intricate. In this book, however, I will focus on the most pertinent and influential factors contributing to this enigma:

Reason #1: The Lies We Tell Ourselves
How Jesus become the best-kept secret in Judaism.

Reason #2: What Was Done to Us in Jesus's Name
Christian antisemitism & replacement theology.

Reason #3: What Christians Tell Us About Our God
Judaism continues to reject the gospel Because It Got Contaminated.

Israel & The Jews: Why Should You Care?

For several reasons! Israel, often referred to as the Holy Land, is regarded as the spiritual heart of Christianity. Primarily, it is the birthplace of Yeshua (Hebrew for "Jesus," meaning salvation), the most renowned Jewish figure in history and the central figure of Christianity. According to the New Testament, Jesus was born in Bethlehem, a small town in the Judean region of Israel. He spent most of his life and ministry in Israel, with significant events like his baptism in the Jordan River, the Sermon on the Mount, and the Last Supper all occurring in Israel.

Additionally, many early events of the Christian Church transpired in Israel. Apostles Peter and Paul, who played crucial roles in spreading Christianity, were both Jews who lived in the region. The Council of Jerusalem, considered a pivotal event in the early history of the Christian Church, also took place in Israel.

Besides its historical and biblical importance, Israel houses numerous holy sites considered sacred by Christians. These include the Church of the Holy Sepulchre in Jerusalem, believed by some to be the site of Jesus' burial and resurrection, and the Garden Tomb, another site some consider Jesus' burial location. The Church of the Nativity in Bethlehem, where Jesus is thought to have been born, is another important place for Christians.

In fact, any avid reader of the Bible will quickly notice the recurring themes within it. "Jerusalem" is mentioned over 800 times in the Scriptures, and "Israel" appears over 2,300 times. Additionally, the epicenter of events is primarily in the land of Israel, with most main characters being Israeli-Jews. The very first Church was in Jerusalem, and its members were predominantly Jews. The apostles were Jews as well. In those days, "Christianity" was a Jewish denomination or movement. As such, one would expect modern Israel to be the most Christian country on earth. I mean, Mecca, the birthplace of Muhammad and Islam, is 99.9% Muslim.

However, modern Israel is vastly different. Today, only 0.05% of

Israel's population consists of Jewish[I] believers in Jesus, and 1.9% are non-Jewish Christians.[II] So, as you can see, Jesus is not welcome here in His own land.

In most parts of the world, the name "Jesus" carries either a positive or neutral connotation. In Islam, Jesus is considered a prophet. In Asia, where there are already millions of gods, adding another deity is not usually an issue. For instance, in Hinduism, the term "deva" refers to deities or celestial beings worshipped as aspects of the divine. Hinduism features many devas, each with distinct forms, attributes, and responsibilities. So, adding one more to their list would likely not be problematic. In the West, even among secular people who may object to Christianity (sometimes for valid reasons), they typically have no issue with Jesus himself. However, in Judaism, there are many preconceived notions about Jesus, and these are overwhelmingly negative.

As you will soon see, there are several historical, religious, and political factors contributing to the current situation. Whatever the reasons, I will argue that behind these reasons lies a spiritual catalyst. I believe that on a cosmic level, nothing is as terrifying to the devil as the idea that Jews will turn to Jesus. Satan knows that once Israel believes, it means "game over" for him (Romans 11). As a result, he will do everything in his power to prevent Jews from accepting Christ. So far, he is doing a great job.

Israel can be likened to God's baton or standard. In the past, the flag carried at the front of a military unit during a war was typically referred to as the unit's "colors" or "standard." These were banners or flags used to identify the unit and serve as a rallying point for the soldiers. In ancient armies, the flag/colors were treated with great respect and considered a symbol of the unit's honor and traditions. In some cases, the colors were carried by a special guard of soldiers responsible for protecting the flag and ensuring it was not captured by the enemy. If the flag fell into enemy hands, it would result in chaos and disrupt the tactics of the army that lost it. In this sense, Israel is God's flag. So when you read about Israel in the scriptures, think of it as God's flag/colors that the enemy seeks to destroy.

[I] Whereby your parents are Jewish.
[II] Of all denominations. About half are Catholics.

Before There Was Israel

In Hebrew, the word representing the act of "making a covenant" also means "excision" or "amputation," implying the involvement of blood. This is also where the English expression "to cut a deal" comes from. When God called Abraham to leave his home and venture into the unknown, He established a covenant with him, promising numerous descendants, land, and authority in return for his faith.

In Genesis 15, God established a covenant with Abraham, incorporating a visual element that Abraham was already familiar with. He instructed Abraham to gather several animals, dissect them in half, and arrange the pieces into two rows with a clear path in the center. This act was known as forming a covenant, with both parties involved walking the path between the dismembered animals to declare their commitment. It was a non-verbal way of saying, "I swear my life on this!"

What makes the covenant in Genesis 15 extraordinary is that God Himself appeared and alone passed between the pieces of the slain animals, staking His life on his promises to Abraham. This one-sided covenant was not contingent on anything Abraham had to do; it was solely up to God. All Abraham had to do was believe. Through this covenant, God conveys that regardless of Abraham's actions, God will always uphold his end of the agreement.

Interestingly, God promised Abraham both a land and a nation. The two (the land of Israel and the nation of Israel) are woven together:

I will make you into a great nation, and I will bless you; I will make your name great, and you will be a blessing. I will bless those who bless you, and whoever curses you I will curse; and all peoples on earth will be blessed through you.
(Genesis 12:2-3)

I will establish my covenant as an everlasting covenant between me and you and your descendants after you for the generations to come, to be your God and the God of your

> *descendants after you. The whole land of Canaan, where you now reside as a foreigner, I will give as an everlasting possession to you and your descendants after you; and I will be their God. (Genesis 17:7-8)*

> *There above it stood the Lord, and he said: 'I am the Lord, the God of your father Abraham and the God of Isaac. I will give you and your descendants the land on which you are lying. Your descendants will be like the dust of the earth, and you will spread out to the west and to the east, to the north and to the south. All peoples on earth will be blessed through you and your offspring. (Genesis 28:13-14)*

These verses, among others, attest that Israel came from Abraham and that God's promise to him is fulfilled through his descendants- the people of Israel.

Centuries later, a vast nation of approximately two million people emerged. As the inhabitants of this nation prepared to enter the land promised to Abraham, God demanded their unwavering obedience. He cautioned them that if they neglected to heed His warnings, other nations would rise against them and expel them from their land (Deuteronomy 28:49). If Israel chooses to worship other gods, the God of Israel won't protect them. This passivity was known to Israel as "God's wrath." Furthermore, God declared that the Israelites' disloyalty would lead to their dispersion to the farthest corners of the earth, where they would dwell as strangers without respite:

> *Then the Lord will scatter you among all nations, from one end of the earth to the other. There you will worship other gods—gods of wood and stone, which neither you nor your ancestors have known. Among those nations you will find no repose, no resting place for the sole of your foot. There the Lord will give you an*

> *anxious mind, eyes weary with longing, and a despairing heart. You will live in constant suspense, filled with dread both night and day, never sure of your life. In the morning you will say, "If only it were evening!" and in the evening, "If only it were morning!"—because of the terror that will fill your hearts and the sights that your eyes will see. (Deuteronomy 28:64-67)*

Since that promise, Israel's sufferings prove that Israel is indeed God's chosen people. However, God also vowed to honor His original covenant and ultimately bring them back to their Land again (Deuteronomy 30:1-10). Despite these admonitions, the Israelites sinned, leading to their exile from their homeland.

In the 8th century BC, the Assyrian Empire invaded Israel, taking many Israelites captive and causing most of Israel's Tribes to disappear. Later, in the 6th century BC, the Babylonian Exile occurred when Nebuchadnezzar invaded Judah, destroyed Jerusalem and the First Temple, and took many Jews captive to Babylon before Persian king Cyrus the Great allowed them to return to Jerusalem and rebuild the temple. During the 2nd century BC, Greek persecution under Antiochus IV Epiphanes led to the Maccabean Revolt, impacting Jewish religious practices.

In the New Testament, Jesus spoke outside the temple and prophesied its destruction (Matthew 24), which came to pass in 70 AD as Jerusalem was destroyed, and about 65 years later, the people of Israel were exiled following the Bar-Kokhba rebellion.

Evidently, Israel did indeed suffer the consequences of her wrongdoing, yet was never entirely destroyed.

Ever since and throughout history, Jews have faced expulsion from numerous countries, such as Spain, Portugal, and England.

However, alongside prophecies of wrath, wars, and attempts to exterminate the Jewish people, God promised that the people of Israel would never be destroyed and would ultimately return to their land:

> *For I will take you [Israel] out of the nations; I will gather you from all the countries and bring you back into your own land. I will sprinkle clean water on you, and you will be clean; I will cleanse you from all your impurities and from all your idols. I will give you a new heart and put a new spirit in you; I will remove from you your heart of stone and give you a heart of flesh. And I will put my Spirit in you and move you to follow my decrees and be careful to keep my laws. Then you will live in the land I gave your ancestors; you will be my people, and I will be your God.*
> *(Ezekiel 36:24-29)*

Likewise, Isaiah prophesied:

> *He will raise a banner for the nations and gather the exiles of Israel; he will assemble the scattered people of Judah from the four quarters of the earth. (Isaiah 11:12)*

What God was doing with Israel served as a banner for the nations. This, I believe, hasn't changed today.

Jeremiah, too, promised that Israel would never cease to exist (Jeremiah 31:35-36). Astonishingly, the Jewish people withstood the relentless assaults of not just one but six superpowers: Egypt, Babylon, Persia, Greece, Rome, and Nazi Germany. Not only did they survive, but they also flourished! And that, in the words of Mark Twain, the Jews did "with their hands tied behind their backs."

Defying all odds and without any natural explanation, the Jewish people continued to exert a disproportionate influence on the world by preserving and transmitting the Word of God, as well as making significant contributions to scientific and medical advancements, literature, art, and more.

For this reason, "Why, the Jews, your Majesty - the Jews!" was the response of the 17th-century French mathematician and theologian Blaise Pascal to King Louis XIV when the king asked him to provide evidence for the existence of God.

Over a century ago, Mark Twain endeavored to unravel the extraordinary existence of the Jews, ultimately finding himself in awe and unable to fully grasp their remarkable resilience and impact:

> *If the statistics are right, the Jews constitute but one quarter of one percent of the human race. It suggests a nebulous puff of star dust lost in the blaze of the Milky Way. Properly, the Jew ought hardly to be heard of, but he is heard of, has always been heard of. He is as prominent on the planet as any other people, and his importance is extravagantly out of proportion to the smallness of his bulk. His contributions to the world's list of great names in literature, science, art, music, finance, medicine and abstruse learning are also very out of proportion to the weakness of his numbers. He has made a marvelous fight in this world in all ages; and has done it with his hands tied behind him. He could be vain of himself and be excused for it. The Egyptians, the Babylonians and the Persians rose, filled the planet with sound and splendor, then faded to dream-stuff and passed away; the Greeks and Romans followed and made a vast noise, and they were gone; other people have sprung up and held their torch high for a time but it burned out, and they sit in twilight now, and have vanished. The Jew saw them all, survived them all, and is now what he always was, exhibiting no decadence, no infirmaties, of age, no weakening of his parts, no slowing of his energies, no dulling of his alert but aggressive mind. All things are mortal but the Jews; all*

> *other forces pass, but he remains. What is the secret of his immortality?[1]*

Mark Twain lived and died before the Holocaust attempted to eliminate the Jewish people. Despite six million Jews dying in Holocaust, the Jews continued to shine in the last 75 years:

> *Jews are a famously accomplished group. They make up 0.2 percent of the world population, but 54 percent of the world chess champions, 27 percent of the Nobel physics laureates and 31 percent of the medicine laureates. Jews make up 2 percent of the U.S. population, but 21 percent of the Ivy League student bodies, 26 percent of the Kennedy Center honorees, 37 percent of the Academy Award-winning directors, 38 percent of those on a recent Business Week list of leading philanthropists, 51 percent of the Pulitzer Prize winners for nonfiction.[2]*

Perhaps even more astounding than Twain's amazement are the words of the individual who seemingly inspired Twain's thoughts, the 19th-century British theologian Charles Spurgeon. Before anyone could even fathom that the people of Israel would once again reside in the Land of Israel, Spurgeon wrote:

> *Israel has now become alienated from her own land. Her sons, though they can never forget the sacred dust of Palestine, yet die at a hopeless distance from her consecrated shores. But it shall not be so forever, for her sons shall again rejoice in her: her land shall be called Beulah, for as a young man marrieth a virgin so shall her sons marry her. "I will place you in your own land," is God's promise to them . . . They are to*

> *have a national prosperity which shall make them famous; nay, so glorious shall they be that Egypt, and Tyre, and Greece, and Rome, shall all forget their glory in the greater splendour of the throne of David . . . If there be anything clear and plain, the literal sense and meaning of this passage [Ezekiel 37:1-10]—a meaning not to be spirited or spiritualized away—must be evident that both the two and the ten tribes of Israel are to be restored to their own land, and that a king is to rule over them.[3]*

Spurgeon's words must have been seen as completely disconnected from reality by his friends. After all, history teaches that people who leave their homeland typically lose their identity within three to five generations. They simply vanish. However, the people of Israel have maintained their identity for thousands of years. While nations such as Moab, Ammon, Edom, and the Philistines, who once fought against Israel, have been wiped off the map, the Jews withstood the test of time.

Based solely on the Holy Scriptures and defying all expectations or logic, Spurgeon astutely recognized that the people of Israel would eventually return to their land. No other nation in history can be compared to Israel, which, despite its modest size and the constant animosity and attempts to eradicate it, has not only endured but also reclaimed its original homeland, as prophesied in the Bible. The very existence of the Jewish people serves as a testament not only to the reality of God but also to His unwavering fidelity to His promises.

The nation of Israel has persevered through thousands of years of conquests, wars, pogroms, crusades, the Holocaust, inquisitions, and exiles. Remarkably, and against all odds, the State of Israel was re-established in the Land of Israel. On May 14, 1948, David Ben-Gurion, the head of the Jewish Agency, proclaimed the establishment of the State of Israel in the Land of Israel. Since then, Jews have returned to their homeland from all corners of the world. My family, for instance, came to Israel from Europe after surviving the Holocaust. Even after the state's founding, Israel has faced numerous challenging wars but has remained unscathed.

Great empires and entire civilizations have either disappeared entirely or been assimilated into other cultures, leaving no trace behind. Yet, the people of Israel have persisted. We never hear about a Swede of Philistine origin, a Russian of Edomite origin, or a Yemeni of Ammonite origin. However, here in Israel, we have Jews of Ethiopian, British, Moroccan, Polish, and many other origins. The nation of Israel continues to exist, and its identity has been preserved.

Concurrently, and founded on the same biblical assurances, the Zionist movement arose. However, much to the astonishment of many, this movement lacked a religious character. From the very first Zionist Congress, a fervent debate emerged among rabbis and ultra-Orthodox Jews who voiced concerns about aligning with the Zionist movement due to its overtly secular nature. Consequently, the people of Israel appeared to forsake the religion of Israel (that is, the orthodox rabbinic version of it) and migrated to Israel, leaving their faith behind in the old continent. This phenomenon sets the stage for a later discussion - the distinction between the people of Israel and the "religion of Israel."

REASON #1:
THE LIES WE TELL OURSELVES

HOW JESUS BECOME THE BEST-KEPT SECRET IN JUDAISM

Israel's Religion

Unlike other religions and cultures, the religion of Israel is unique in that it has always been an ethnic religion. This means that the ethno-national and religious aspects are "virtually inseparable,"[4] as noted by Prof. Mordechai Altshuler. This can be seen in Israel's holidays, where national and religious dimensions are intertwined and are celebrated today by all Jews, secular and atheist included.

Until the end of the Second Temple period, the term "religion" related to the commandments of the Torah (Law of Moses). A person's Jewishness was not determined by the extent of their religiosity but by their genealogical origin, inherited from their parents. A Jewish individual could be ethnically Jewish but an apostate in the religion of Israel. In other words, I, Eitan, am Jewish because my parents and grandparents are Jews. Yet because I believe in Yeshua-Jesus, I am considered an apostate by religious Orthodox Jews. But to understand this, we must go back.

During the first centuries, as part of the Pharisee[1] sect's efforts to dominate Judaism and eliminate other Jewish movements, their Sages taught that concerning one's identity, the religious-theological aspect was superior to the national-ethnic one. Consequently, a Jew would be considered as such only if they aligned with the theological beliefs of the Sages of Halachic-rabbinic (pharisaic) Judaism. Those who deviated risked losing their Jewish identity. In fact, the Talmud refers to these individuals with derogatory labels such as "nations," "heretics," "sects," etc.

Prof. Avraham Melamed explains[5] that the meaning of 'religion' transformed throughout Jewish history. He argues that Pharisaic-rabbinic Judaism has, from its beginning, leaned towards the idea that Jewish identity is based on observing the commandments of the rabbinic Oral Law (or, Oral Torah; the rabbinic traditions) of the

---

[1] The Pharisees were a Jewish religious movement and a school of thought in Israel during the time of Second Temple Judaism. They would often come into conflict with Jesus.

rabbinic sages rather than on an individual's ethnicity.[6] In his book, "Religion: From Law to Belief," Melamed presents evidence that the shift undertaken by rabbinic Judaism occurred concurrently with and perhaps inspired by, the development of the Jewish-Christian faith.

This raises the question: does Judaism have a systematic theology?

But first, it is essential to clarify what is "Judaism." In contrast with today, where Judaism means the rabbinic-halachic-pharisaic system of belief, no single, unified form of "Judaism" existed during the Second Temple Period. Instead, multiple forms of Judaism coexisted,[7] with various factions competing to influence the people of Israel. However, most Jews did not affiliate with these factions (Pharisees, Sadducees, Essenes, etc.). For the majority, religious life centered on observing the Torah, worshiping at the Temple during the pilgrimage festivals, and following a rabbi of their liking.

The destruction of the Second Temple marked the end of that colorful version of Judaism, paving the way for the Pharisees and their successors—the Sages of Oral Law (or rabbis of Orthodox Judaism.)[II] With the temple gone and Sadducee priests rendered jobless, control of religious institutions gradually shifted to the Pharisaic rabbis. As a result, only two Jewish movements survived the Temple's destruction: that of the Christian Jews or Jewish followers of Jesus, who functioned without political aspirations, and that of Rabbinic Judaism, established by the Pharisees as a political faction aiming to dominate the Jewish world in both its spiritual-religious and political-economic spheres.

As an interesting side note, in the Talmud, Yoma 39b, Jewish Sages described mysterious omens occurring at the temple beginning approximately 40 years before its destruction (around 30 AD). These omens included the western candle burning out, the lot for the sacrificial goat on Yom Kippur always being black rather than white, and the temple doors opening on their own. These phenomena caused great concern among the religious leaders, who believed God was no longer confirming the acceptance of the annual sacrifice. One particularly significant event was the "strip of crimson wool" that stopped turning from red to white, which the priests believed was evidence that God had abandoned the temple. Rabbi Avraham Stav stated, "It means that the temple ceased to exist as a place that

---

[II] Rabbinic, Halachic, and Orthodox Judaism are all one and the same, originating from the Pharisees, who managed to take over Judaism.

inspires the Divine Spirit."[8]

Interestingly, these omens, interpreted as signs of God leaving the temple, coincided with the date of the crucifixion of Jesus of Nazareth. What a coincidence!

Returning to our question, do religious Jews engage in theology? A well-known adage states: "Christianity has a theology; Judaism has the Oral Law."[9] This suggests that the rabbinic tradition lacks theology and focuses solely on the mitzvot (commandments of the rabbis). Such a perspective contends that a fundamental difference between Judaism and Christianity is partly reflected by the practice and study of theology.[10] This view regards the commandments of the Torah, including those of the Oral Torah and its traditions, as the primary, perhaps the sole, element of the Rabbinic Jewish religion.[11]

Conversely, studies attempting to analyze the essence of Judaism cannot disregard the fact that Rabbinic Judaism does, in fact, embodies a particular systematic theology, often referred to as "principles of faith," "foundations of the religion," or "core values."[12] Any Jew who rejects this theology essentially excludes themselves from Judaism.[13] This aspect is not that different from Christianity.[III]

Jewish scholar Gershom Scholem posits that the theology created by the followers of Christ emerged simultaneously with the development of rabbinic theology, the origins of which can be traced back to the compilation of the Mishnah.[IV]

In this case, the claim that (rabbinic) Judaism lacks theology is unfounded; instead, it possesses a well-defined theology distinct from its "Christian" counterpart. In fact, as we will soon see, a pillar in the systematic Jewish theology is rejecting the core of Christianity, rejecting Jesus Christ. This is why, today, you are allowed to be Jewish and Buddhist ("Jewbu") or deny the existence of God altogether (secular Jew) and still be Jewish. However, you can't believe in Jesus and be Jewish.

Some scholars assert that the version of Judaism conceived by the Pharisee's sages established a new category of Jews characterized by differences in doctrine and theology. They argue that as the rabbis

---

[III] Many denominations in Christianity will have a set of core theological values that one must profess to be considered a "truly saved believer."

[IV] The Mishnah is the first significant written compilation of Jewish oral traditions, known as the Oral Torah. It was assembled over about 130 years during the first and second centuries AD.

transformed Judaism from ethnicity to theology, a distinct and novel form of religion emerged, replacing the Jewish classism that typified the Second Temple period with halachic orthodoxy. Thereby, Jews who express incorrect beliefs can no longer be considered Israel.[14]

Professor Menachem Kellner cites the great Maimonides ("Rambam"; Rabbi Moses Ben-Maimon [1138-1204], a famous Jewish theologian) as someone who truly grasped the theological revolution initiated by the Sages:

> *According to Maimonides' view, an individual born to a Jewish parent is not considered a Jew until they consciously accept the fundamental tenets of Judaism...[15] Maimonides posited that Judaism is, or should be, based on systematic theology. As the most significant and audacious Jewish theologian in the Middle Ages, he possessed not only the keen intellect to propose such a theology but also the courage to confront the full implications of his stance...[16] For Maimonides, not all Israel is the true Israel, and the answer to the question 'Who is a Jew?' is clear:* **the one who adheres to the Oral Law** *and observes its commandments, whether minor or major.[17]*

We can infer that similar to the theological studies in Christian seminaries, dogmatic theology is also explored in Yeshivas, where Jewish students immerse themselves in the rabbinic Oral Law. Both represent two competing interpretations of the Bible, both deriving authority from it and aiming to offer a theological alternative to the long-gone Levitical sacrifices in the post-Temple era. Professor Israel Yuval effectively illustrates this concept by discussing the evolving tradition surrounding the Passover holiday:

> *After the Temple's destruction in 70 AD, two competing interpretations of Passover emerged: Halachic Judaism centered the holiday on the*

story of redemption in Egypt, a model for the future redemption, while Jesus' followers presented the story of the ultimate redemption achieved through the Messiah's blood and the anticipation of his second coming. Both narratives offered a liturgical replacement for sacrifice and addressed a holiday of redemption during a period of destruction and subjugation to monarchies. The similarity between these two religions, or these competing currents, was particularly pronounced in the first centuries AD when they faced a common challenge - idolatry.[18]

The above analysis suggests that the early version of Christianity and Rabbinic Judaism are simply two currents originating from the same stream of Second Temple Judaism and the historical circumstances of that era. These two religions, or paths, are faith-based and diverge in terms of doctrine and theology.[19] Prof. Israel Yuval suggested that Judaism and Christianity were, in fact, like twin babies in the womb.[20] Maimonides concordant with the Sages' view, whereby a Jew is not born Jewish; rather, a Jew is born with the potential to become Jewish if they are nurtured and educated to be one. They must strive to maintain this identity throughout their life by adhering to the commandments and traditions of the rabbinic Oral Law.[21] Again, this is much like Christianity, whereby the believer must confess certain doctrines and, in some cases, keep some laws, customs, or traditions to be a true Christian.

Jacob Yadgar, Professor of Israel Studies at the University of Oxford, pointed out that Jewish identity isn't inherently evident according to the rabbinic tradition. Instead, individuals must continually uphold and reaffirm their identity by observing the commandments of the Oral Law.[22]

The Sages believed that observing the Oral Law (rabbinic traditions) was fundamental to Jewish identity; as a result, they viewed rejecting the traditions of the Oral Law as equivalent to forsaking Judaism altogether. In other words, you can't be Jewish unless you surrender to the rabbis and the rabbinic theology. The core of their theology is the rejection of Jesus Christ.

This shift represents the transition from 'ethnos' to 'ethos'—from an ethnic Judaism based on origin to a religion defined by adherence to rabbinical law. Prof. Adiel Shermer explains that the theological "reformation" of the Sages was groundbreaking because, for the first time in Israel's history, an individual's Jewish identity was determined by the practices/tradition they followed:

> *At the same time, the sages also began to determine the boundaries of Jewish identity by excluding Jews who did not agree with them by 'marking' them with the label 'MINIM' [species], and by establishing a halachic prohibition on social and economic contacts with them... In this way, the boundaries of Jewish identity were determined according to the way of the sages.*[23]

Ever since, and to this day, "MINIM" mainly refers to Jewish followers of Jesus. Those who consent to the decrees of the Oral Law are in; those who dare to look outside will find themselves rejected by Judaism. Prof. Kellner added: "He who is incapable of this [adhering to the rabbinic Oral Law] or is mistaken in the matter is not considered an inferior Jew but a non-Jew."[24] In other words, if you are a Jewish follower of Jesus, you are not just wrong in your Messiahology. As far as the rabbis are concerned, you are no longer considered a Jew.

The 'Shulchan Aruch'[IV] also continued in this trend, determining that whoever rejects the rabbinic Oral Law removes themselves from the nation of Israel and must be treated as an apostate.[25] When the Sages achieved the necessary level of authority, they began to determine the boundaries of Jewish identity by excluding Jews who did not agree to submit to their ideology.[26] In the context of that era, this mainly affected the Jewish followers of Jesus. This emphasis on the religious-theological aspect over the national-ethnic one was carried out with a clear intention by the Sages to establish themselves as the gatekeepers of the Jewish world, to turn their sect into the one

---

[V] The most widely consulted of the various legal codes in Judaism. It was authored in Safed by Joseph Karo in 1563.

and only "true" Judaism, and to get rid of the Christian-Jews.

The ramifications of this religious reformation, which led to a person's Jewishness being determined by their religious commitment to Orthodox Judaism rather than their DNA, were significant. This granted the rabbis dominion over the Jewish spiritual realm, which came with much power. From then on, those who embraced the Halachic/rabbinic religion would be considered "kosher" Jews. At the same time, the Jewishness of apostates under their jurisdiction would be scrutinized. The most extreme aspect of this reform implies that a Jew isn't born a Jew but is only born with the potential to become one by accepting the authority of the rabbinic Oral Law and studying it adequately.[27] So anyone wanting to be Jewish must first join a Yeshiva, where he will be indoctrinated with rabbinic theology. This is, of course, circular reasoning,[VI] and the cornerstone of that theology is the rejection of Christ.

The Foundation of Rabbinic Judaism: the Oral Law

We believe that when Moses brought the Written Law down, he did not only bring with him the Written Law but also the Oral Law. We believe that the Written and Oral Torah were brought down together. Thus they must not be separated.[28] (Rabbi Rami Brachiahu)

There is no doubt that the authority of the Oral Law is exclusive. Only those who believe in the Oral Law possess the Written Law. And anyone denying the Oral Law does not have the Written Law.[29] (Rabbi Daniel Assor)

Jews never followed the literal words of the Written Law but rather the traditions of the rabbis.[30] (Rabbi Chaim Schimmel)

[VI] Circular reasoning is a logical fallacy in which the reasoner begins with what they are trying to end with.

The term 'Torah' can be confusing as sometimes it means "Law," referring to the commandments given by Moses, while other times referring to the first five books of the Bible (the Pentateuch). However, you may not be as familiar with the term 'Oral Torah' or 'Oral Law,' which, in Hebrew, signifies "the Torah that is orally transmitted." Also known as the Mishna, a term derived from the Hebrew verb meaning to recite. The Oral Torah embodies an essential aspect of Jewish belief. According to Jewish tradition, it was transmitted verbally until about the third century, following the belief that God conveyed the Oral Torah to Moses orally, who then communicated it to the elder orally, and so on and so forth. The Oral Torah aims to offer comprehensive instructions on implementing the laws in the Written Torah. It also comprises countless commentaries, traditions, and Mitzvot, all of which are considered vital complements to the Written Torah. This vast body of knowledge is believed to have been passed down orally through generations.

According to the Jewish folktale, writing down the Oral Law was forbidden. Instead, people memorized and recited it to each other. However, after the Second Temple's destruction in 70 AD, the Jewish people were expelled from Jerusalem and dispersed among other nations. Fearing that the essence, traditions, and teachings of Judaism would be lost, Rabbi Judah ha-Nasi decided to break with tradition and write down the Oral Law to preserve it. Judah ha-Nasi, a second-century rabbi, chief redactor, and editor of the Mishnah, organized the teachings into six orders. Each order dealt with an area of God's law, such as agriculture, the Temple and holy things, purification, women-related issues, personal damages, and holy festivals. These were divided into 60 tractates, then into chapters containing individual "Mishnas."

The six orders of the Mishna form the basis of the Talmud, with the rest being commentary. Following the first codification of the Mishna, several respected rabbis and sages added explanations, clarifications, and additions over the years. This process led to the "Gemara," an exposition of the Mishna. Subsequent explanations, discussions, and additions were later incorporated.

The Talmud's pages display the initial stages of the Mishna and Gemara in a central column, with later commentaries in surrounding thinner columns. This enormous collective body of writings, including the central Mishna and Gemara and surrounding rabbinic commentary, forms the Talmud. Two versions exist: the "Jerusalem Talmud," compiled by Israel-based rabbis, and the more prevalent and more respected, the "Babylonian Talmud," developed by Jewish rabbis in Babylon following the destruction of the Second Temple. The latter is typically referred to when discussing the "Oral Law."

The exile was instrumental for the Pharisees, allowing them to finally and fully integrate their theology absent the priesthood, Temple, and Jerusalem. These elements had previously obstructed their influence in Judaism. However, in exile, the Pharisees could shape Judaism's theology and future, resulting in the predominance of Rabbinic Judaism.

A substantial portion of the Talmud addresses how to adhere to the law without the Temple, generally advocating for set morning and evening prayers to replace sacrifices. Essentially, the Talmud removes the necessity for priests and a temple, removing the need for the Written Law.

In Mark chapter 7, we see that many additional laws and traditions had already been well-established when Jesus started his ministry. The Pharisees and some teachers of the law gathered around Jesus, criticizing his disciples for eating with defiled, unwashed hands, which went against the tradition of the elders. Jesus responded by quoting Isaiah, accusing the Pharisees of honoring God with their lips but having hearts far from him, worshiping in vain, and teaching mere human rules. He then chastised them for holding onto human traditions instead of obeying God's commands.

Thus, as a Jewish follower of Jesus, I can attest that the Talmud includes numerous wise, helpful, and beautiful writings. Still, I do not consider them divinely inspired.

Prof. Avigdor Shinan, a Jewish expert on rabbinic literature at the Hebrew University in Jerusalem, sums up the Oral Law in this way:[31]

> *I am a professor at the Hebrew University in Jerusalem. I specialize in post-Bible Jewish literature, i.e., anything written after the 2nd century BC: Mishna, Talmud, Siddur Prayer, including Midrash and translations for the Bible. All Jewish history, known as "rabbinic literature," – is the milestone of Judaism, not the*

> Bible. Our current theology is not that of the Bible. The rules that we abide by today are not the rules defined in the Bible, but rather those set forth by our sages… The Jewish Oral Law – the laws of the Sabbath, Kosher, and anything else you may think of – is not derived from the Bible. The Bible does not mention a "synagogue," there is no such thing as "Kadish," there is no "Kol Nidrei" [Jewish prayers], "Bar Mitzvah," or "praying shawl." When someone defines something as "Jewish" and begins to search after its roots – they will not find it in the Bible, but rather in the literature of our sages – that's where it all began.

As if to make things confusing, the rabbis began referring to both the "Written Torah" and the "Oral Torah" collectively as simply "the Torah." This convergence causes the Jewish people to often quote from the literature of the rabbinic Oral Torah under the impression that they're citing the Written Torah. The intentional blurring of these lines has effectively amalgamated the two, causing confusion about their distinct origins and content. With this genius move, the mission to take over Judaism became effortless.

For instance, religious Jews often tell me that "the Torah documents that Jesus admitted to being punished in hell in boiling excrement," not knowing it's actually a story in the Talmud.[32]

The Imposition of Rabbinic Judaism

Over time, Jewish sages gained supreme power, similar to that of the Catholic Pope. They achieved this by teaching that the Oral Law, which they propagated, had existed forever. According to their teachings, the Oral Law was not only handed down to Moses on Mt. Sinai but was also known and followed by Abraham[33] and Isaac,[34] a claim that raises several logical and theological contradictions.[VII]

[VII] I expand on these contradictions in "The New Kings of Israel: A Theological Survey and Critique of Rabbinic Judaism."

Furthermore, they asserted that God Himself sits and recites the Oral Torah[35] in his Beth Midrash (school)[36] just like any other Yeshiva student whose primary focus was the study of the Talmud.

The sages gained enormous power and influence through such declarations, enabling them to reshape Judaism. They issued statements like "the words of the sages are better than those of the Written Law"[37] and "stricter are the words of the sages than those of the prophets," arguing that while the Written Law contained both prohibitions and permissions, the words of the sages were universally strict. Moreover, Rabbi Akiva expounded that Jews must be in awe of God and the sages alike.[38]

The rabbis slowly began to equate their status with that of God.[39] They claimed authority, becoming the new kings of Israel: "Who is my king? My rabbi!"[40] Every student was ordered to "respect his rabbi more than his father,"[41] to "obey the words of the sages,"[42] and to "drink in their words with thirst."[43] Challenging them was not an option either, as "anyone disobeying the words of the sages must be put to death,"[44] and "anyone who mocks the words of the Sages will be sentenced to boiling excrement"[45] in the afterlife.

The Cosmic Power Shift

If earlier I mentioned how the sages were first puzzled by the fact God stopped confirming his acceptance of Israel's sacrifices at the temple, the destruction of the Temple catalyzed a significant shift in authority, as illustrated by a well-known story in the Talmud, Bava Metzia 59b. This narrative underscores how the authority of the rabbis began to supersede that of God, signifying a transference of divine sovereignty to the sages.

According to the Talmudic tale, a Jewish man named Akhnai sought to enlarge his clay oven. He disassembled it into tiles and restructured it with sand. A question was then posed to the Sanhedrin: was the newly reassembled oven pure or impure? According to the Talmud, Rabbi Eliezer provided numerous arguments asserting the oven's purity. Nonetheless, the majority of the Sanhedrin sages rejected his conclusions, maintaining that the oven was impure.

Unfazed, Rabbi Eliezer used supernatural phenomena to defend his standpoint and prove God was on his side. Miracles involving a translocated fig tree and an uphill water stream were invoked. When these demonstrations failed to convince his peers, he again appealed to the heavens for support:

> *Rabbi Eliezer then said to them: If the halakha is in accordance with my opinion, Heaven will prove it. A Divine Voice emerged from Heaven and said: Why are you differing with Rabbi Eliezer, as the halakha is in accordance with his opinion in every place that he expresses an opinion?*[46]

God affirmed Rabbi Eliezer's claim by sending an echo from the sky. Yet despite this divine endorsement, Rabbi Yehoshua boldly contested with the most significant proclamation in the Talmud and Jewish history:

> *Rabbi Yehoshua stood on his feet and said: It is written: "It is not in heaven" (Deuteronomy 30:12). The Gemara asks: What is the relevance of the phrase "It is not in heaven" in this context? Rabbi Yirmeya says: Since the Torah was already given at Mount Sinai, we do not regard a Divine Voice.*[47]

In essence, God no longer had the ultimate control; the jurisdiction now belonged to the rabbis, who held ultimate power to discern right and wrong:

> *Since the majority of Rabbis disagreed with Rabbi Eliezer's opinion, the halakha is not ruled in accordance with his opinion.*[48]

The story ends with God's voice being heard one last time:

> *The Holy One, Blessed be He, smiled and said: My children have triumphed over Me; My children have triumphed over Me.*[49]

God conceded to the rabbis' authority, acknowledging that their rulings superseded His and Moses' own. This was a pivotal moment for Israel. Since then, God ceased to reveal Himself to His people in the way He had throughout the Bible. From that point onwards, according to the rabbinic narrative, God's will was manifested solely through the halachic sages - the rabbis themselves.

This Talmudic tale, which established the basis for rabbinical authority, highlights the issue of "circular reasoning." It begs the question: Where does the claim to rabbinical authority stem? The answer is found within the very narrative crafted by the rabbis themselves.

If the Talmudic legends are not convincing enough, the sages imposed the Oral Law on the people through coercion and threats of death, ensuring that the common people would accept the Oral Law without question. Maimonides wrote:

> *A person who does not acknowledge the validity of the Oral Law is not the rebellious elder mentioned in the Written Law. Instead, he is one of the heretics and he should be put to death by any person. Since it has become known that such a person denies the Oral Law, he may be pushed into a pit and may not be helped out. He is like all the rest of the heretics who say that the Written Law is not Divine in origin, those who inform on their fellow Jews and the apostates. All of these are not considered as members of the Jewish people. There is no need for witnesses, a warning, or judges for them to be executed. Instead, whoever kills them performs a great mitzvah and removes an obstacle from people at large.[50]*

There can be no rabbinic Judaism without the Talmud (Oral Law), and the Oral Law cannot exist without rabbis to teach it. Thereby, "rejecting the Oral Law poses the greatest threat to Rabbinic Judaism."[51]

Dismissing the credibility of the Oral Law equates to undermining the foundation of the Halachic-rabbinic sages. Therefore, it is unsurprising that the sages sought to elevate the status of the Oral Law. In doing so, they promoted their own status and demanded respect reserved for kings[52] and even God Himself.[53] Their rulings are deemed more important than the words of the prophets,[54] as a rabbi is considered more distinguished than a prophet.[55] Based on this view, they permitted themselves to threaten that anyone who disputes their rulings would face execution in this world and punishment in the afterlife.[56] The power is solely in their hands.

However, suppose the Oral Law does not originate from God. In that case, the supreme authority the rabbis granted themselves — including their staunch rejection of Jesus Christ — is based on falsehood.

Refuting the rabbinic Oral Law as God-inspired was my doctorate thesis. In the past few years, I have published books, debated rabbis, and released several videos debunking the Oral Law.

Now you can appreciate why a rabbi claimed I'm the biggest threat to rabbinic Judaism since Paul, as no one before took on the mission to discredit the authority of the rabbis and the Oral Law the way I did. However, this comes with a high cost![VIII]

Jesus Challenged the Rabbinic Authority

As you now read the New Testament, it will be much more apparent why Jesus was such a massive threat to the religious establishment of his time, and the Pharisees in particular, as his teachings and actions challenged the authority of the Oral Law.

For instance, one of the points of contention between Jesus and the rabbis concerned the observance of the Sabbath, a day of rest and worship. The Oral Torah prescribed strict guidelines for Sabbath observance, prohibiting activities such as lighting a fire, cooking, or carrying a burden. However, Jesus questioned these rigid interpretations and insisted that the Sabbath was made for humanity's benefit, to serve us, not to burden us. He demonstrated this by healing the sick on the Sabbath and allowing his disciples to pluck

---

[VIII] This brought on me severe persecution, including death threats and other means of intimidation and terrorization. Unfortunately, many in the Messianic Movement were also upset with me for "shaking the status quo" and upsetting the rabbis. Unfortunately, my videos debunking the Oral Law, including the famous debate, were removed from the internet.

grain to eat, both considered violations of the Oral Law.

The Oral Torah emphasized the importance of ritual purity, requiring frequent handwashing and other purification rituals. Jesus criticized these practices as superficial and hypocritical, arguing that true purity came from the heart, not external actions. He famously declared that it was not what entered a person's mouth that defiled them but rather what came out of it – a direct challenge to the Oral Law.

Jesus often confronted the religious leaders who held considerable power and authority due to their expertise in the Law. He denounced their hypocrisy and self-righteousness, accusing them of burdening the people with numerous rules and regulations while neglecting more important matters such as justice, mercy, and faithfulness. In doing so, Jesus challenged the very basis of their authority, asserting that adherence to the rabbinic traditions was not the path to righteousness.

While the Oral Law focused on meticulous observance of rituals and regulations, Jesus emphasized the importance of love, mercy, and compassion. He taught that the two greatest commandments were to love God and love one's neighbor. This was a radical departure from the legalistic mindset fostered by the Oral Law, which prioritized strict adherence to rules and traditions over empathy and compassion. The appeal of Jesus' message made it more likely that people would choose to follow him rather than the teachings of the Pharisees. This increased popularity placed Jesus at odds with the religious establishment, who saw him as threatening their authority and power. Clearly, the scribes and Pharisees had no inclination to accept Jesus' messianic status. Concerned about losing their control, they had no choice but to reject Jesus and employ every means at their disposal to persuade the people of Israel that Jesus was a false prophet and an adversary to their nation.

Before we continue, I understand that the information you have read (and will read) might feel a bit overwhelming, so let's take a moment to clarify a critical point. In modern Judaism, not every Jew adheres strictly to rabbinic teachings. Indeed, the majority of Jews fall into the categories of secular or traditional Judaism. These individuals might not have extensive knowledge about the intricacies of Judaism. Instead, they often follow the teachings of rabbis blindly. They might not be fully aware of historical developments or Jesus's teachings. As such, their perspective of Jesus is primarily shaped by the historical lens, leading to a general rejection of him as the Messiah. We'll delve more into this in the subsequent discussion under reason number two.

For further discussion on the Oral Law, Judaism, the rabbis, and the Talmud, I invite you to read my previously published book, "Rabbinic Judaism Debunked: Debunking the Myth of Rabbinic Oral Law."

Rabbinic Judaism vs. Christian Judaism

"I am the blank page between the Old and the New Testament." [57] *(Sir Benjamin D'Israeli, a Jewish Prime Minister of Great Britain and a believer in Jesus)*

In the first century, the distinction between Jews and Christians was not as clear-cut as it is today. Christianity initially emerged as a Jewish movement from within Judaism, with many early followers, including Jesus and his disciples, being Jews. During this time, Jewish followers of Jesus, or "Jewish-Christians," continued to observe Jewish laws and holidays while embracing Jesus as the Messiah. In fact, the primary debate was whether Gentiles should be allowed to join and follow the Jewish Messiah. Over time, thousands of Gentiles did join, causing theological frictions that are documented in the New Testament.

In the first century or two, Jewish-Christians and other Jews worshipped together in the same Jewish synagogues[58,59] as the split between Judaism and Christianity had not yet been fully realized. Jewish-Christians attended synagogues to pray, hear the Hebrew Bible being read, and participate in discussions on religious matters. However, as the belief in Jesus as the Messiah and the Christian movement gained traction, tensions between Jewish-Christians and other Jews began.

Gradually, the differences in beliefs and practices between Jewish-Christians and mainstream Jews caused tension between the groups. This was solidified by events like the destruction of the Second Temple in 70 AD and especially the failed Bar-Kokhba Revolt in 132-135 CE. Simon Bar-Kokhba led the Second Jewish Revolt against the Romans in 132 AD. At the onset of the rebellion, Jewish followers of Jesus initially supported the revolt against the Romans, viewing it as a defense of the Land of Israel and a fight against oppression. However, a turning point occurred when Rabbi Akiva announced Simon Bar-Kokhba, a warrior known for his extreme cruelty, as the Messiah. This declaration forced Jewish believers in Jesus to withdraw from the rebellion, as they could not accept Bar-Kokhba as the Messiah.

In response to their withdrawal, Rabbi Akiva, in collaboration with the Sanhedrin, devised a comprehensive list of regulations as retaliation in order to excommunicate the Jewish disciples of Jesus from Rabbinic Judaism and prohibit contact between them and the general Jewish population. The situation escalated when the Sanhedrin also resolved to expel all Jewish followers of Jesus from the synagogues. To achieve this, they introduced the "Blessing of the Species" into the Amidah, an eighteen-blessing prayer recited by Jews three times daily in synagogues.

Jewish historian Prof. Katsia Aviali-Tabibian explains:

> *The "Blessing of the Species," which is, in fact, a curse, targets all Christians or, according to some interpretations, specifically Jewish-Christians. These Jewish-Christians were Jews who believed in Jesus as the Messiah but continued to worship alongside other Jews in the synagogues. The purpose of this particular blessing was to alienate and repel them, preventing their influence on the broader Jewish community.*[60]

This became a defining moment, a line drawn in the sand. From then on, Jewish-Christians found themselves estranged, unable to maintain their previous connections within the broader Jewish community could no longer worship in synagogues with other Jews.

Jesus in the Rabbinic Oral Torah

By the third century AD, rabbis attempted to further separate Jesus' disciples from mainstream Judaism by introducing a controversial legend into the Oral Law. They hoped this legend would create discomfort among Jesus' followers and ultimately create animosity between rabbinic Jews and Christian-Jews, expelling the latter from Jewish communities altogether. This legend, found in the Talmud's tractate Sanhedrin 107b, claims that Jesus practiced witchcraft and lured the Israelites away from the God of Israel towards idolatry. According to the story, Jesus was a student of Rabbi Joshua Ben-Perahiah, with whom he had a dispute. In retaliation, Jesus allegedly studied witchcraft in Egypt, intending to corrupt the people of Israel.

However, this legend, authored by rabbis centuries after Jesus' crucifixion, lacks any foundation outside the Talmud and displays a glaring chronological inconsistency. Rabbi Joshua Ben-Perahiah lived and taught in the second century BC, long before Jesus' birth. Prof. Avigdor Shinan comments on this discrepancy, pointing to the implausibility of Jesus being Joshua Ben-Perahiah's disciple due to living in different eras:

> *During his (Joshua Ben-Perahia) escape to Egypt, he was joined by one of his disciples, Jesus (yes indeed, the father of Christianity, although it is chronologically impossible!).*[61]

Another account involving Jewish believers in Jesus appears in tractate Avodah Zara 17, which details a conversation between Rabbi Eliezer and Rabbi Akiva about a Jesus follower named Jacob of Sechania. Known for his ability to heal in Jesus' name, Jacob, a Jewish believer in Jesus, is later mentioned in a story where Rabbi Ishmael's nephew is bitten by a snake. Though Jacob offers to heal the nephew using Jesus' name, Rabbi Ishmael, aware of the miraculous healing powers ascribed to Jesus' disciples, declines the offer, allowing his nephew to die instead.

In the Talmud's tractate, Gittin 56b-57a, another account referencing Jesus, describes him enduring eternal punishment in hell, submerged in boiling animal excrement. This punishment is presented as retribution for his alleged misdeeds and for supposedly leading the people of Israel away from the Torah and towards idolatry.

These intriguing legends underscore the contentious relationship between Jewish believers in Jesus and rabbinic Judaism.

As you can see, rejecting Jesus Christ – declaring him a false

Messiah – became a core value in rabbinic Judaism and one of the primary pillars of Jewish theology. Fast forward two thousand years, and the core of Judaism still seems to revolve around the rejection of Christ.

This is why nowadays we hear prominent Jewish leaders like Rabbi Aaron Moss declaring, "A Jew can believe in Jesus, just as much as a vegetarian can enjoy a steak."[62] However, such statements are mere propaganda and manipulation. Most Jews forget – or are simply unaware - that Jesus, the central figure of the New Testament, was himself Jewish. He taught the Jewish Scriptures, and his followers were also Jewish. They celebrated Jewish holidays and lived in Israel, not Babylon. The New Testament, authored by Jews, chronicles the lives of Jewish people in the land of Israel. This contrasts with the Talmud, which was primarily composed in Babylon, with its central figure being Rabbi Akiva—a descendant of Gentile converts to Judaism from the lineage of Sisera.[63] Ironically, much like Akiva, Rabbinic Judaism shares little in common with the original biblical faith. At the same time, the greatest Jew of all is rejected and considered a stranger.

Turning Pagan

Ashkenazi and Sephardic Jews are two primary cultural subgroups within Judaism, each with its own distinct traditions, practices, and historical experiences. The differences between these groups lie mainly in their historical origins, traditions, and liturgy, including religious customs and practices.

Ashkenazi Jews trace their ancestry to Jewish communities that lived in Western Europe, around modern-day Germany and France, in the early Middle Ages. Following persecutions, Ashkenazi Jews spread throughout Central and Eastern Europe.

Sephardic Jews, on the other hand, are descendants of the Jews from the Iberian Peninsula (Spain and Portugal). After the expulsion of Jews from Spain in 1492 and Portugal in 1497, Sephardic Jews migrated to West Asia (mainly Iraq, Iran, Morocco, and Iman), North Africa, the Ottoman Empire (including modern-day Turkey, Greece, and the Balkans), and the Middle East.

While all Jews base their practices on the Talmud, differences in traditions and practices arose due to the different geographic and cultural contexts of Ashkenazi and Sephardic Jews.

Over the centuries, different philosophical and religious movements have been more prevalent in one group than the other. For instance, the Hasidic movement is an Ashkenazi phenomenon, while the Kabbalistic (mystic) is largely Sephardic.

The development of rabbinic Judaism, especially Sephardic, did not go in a biblical direction; instead, it adopted many pagan beliefs and rituals. In fact, while modern Judaism is not about a relationship with God but about keeping practices and traditions, rabbinic Judaism (again, mostly Sephardic) integrated many pagan rituals and beliefs.

For instance, reincarnation is a central doctrine in Judaism, found in mystical texts such as the Zohar, and is embraced by most branches of Judaism.[64] However, the idea of reincarnation is also found in many pagan and Eastern religions, which raises questions about its place in monotheistic Judaism. Some rabbis use the idea of reincarnation to cultivate fear in their congregants, as seen in the case of a prominent rabbi and member of the Israeli parliament who stated that "immodest women get breast cancer, reincarnate as cows."[65]

Amulets and charms, such as the Mezuzah[66] or the Hamsa,[67] are believed to offer protection or bring good fortune and are widely used by Jews. In fact, last month, when a Jewish friend was severely ill and hospitalized, her mother's rabbi suggested that they replace their Mezuzah for better protection and quicker healing.

Kaddish, a Jewish prayer for the deceased's soul, is recited in memory of the dead and for their soul to transcend into heaven.[68] It is also a known pagan ritual.

Lighting candles is another significant Jewish ritual, often done in memory of the dead and for Sabbath and holidays.[69] However, when Ethiopian Jews returned to Israel after over two thousand years in exile, they were unfamiliar with this ritual and surprised to see Jews making fire so close to the Sabbath.[70]

Grave soaking, also known as "grave lying," is a widespread Jewish practice in Israel. It involves lying on the graves of deceased sages and rabbis to absorb their alleged "spiritual energy."[71] However, this practice is forbidden in the Torah (Numbers 19:16).

In Judaism, the Dough Offering, or Challah Offering, involves setting aside and burning a portion of dough when baking bread to receive divine blessings.[72]

Veneration of dead religious figures, objects, and places is also common in Judaism. It may take the form of praying over the graves of revered rabbis or hanging large paintings of deceased rabbis on the living room walls to bless the house and its residents. This, too, was popular in pagan nations.[73]

Tefillin, or phylacteries, is a small black box containing a scroll with verses. They are worn on the forehead and arm during morning prayers. Wearing amulets or charms for protection was common in various pagan cultures long before Judaism.[74]

Other pagan rituals, such as spells, astrology, luck, breaking glasses against evil spirits, and more, can also be found in rabbinic Judaism.[1]

Coincidently, today as I write these lines, is the eve of Lag BaOmer, a festive day on the Jewish calendar that celebrates the passing of the great sage and mystic rabbi Shimon Bar-Yochai.[75] However, Lag BaOmer customs may appear reminiscent of pagan practices, as many Jews visit his grave, offer prayers at this site, light bonfires, and chant and dance around the fire. This holiday is widely celebrated by Israeli Jews, including young children in schools and as part of municipal events.

Evidently, not only rabbinic Judaism took over Judaism and expel its own Messiah, but it also brought forth many pagan rituals and idolatry.

The Remnant

While rabbinic Judaism managed to overcome and eliminate most other Jewish sects, one group, despite its small size, has survived until now.

In his letter to the Romans, Paul speaks of the "remnant" (11:5), a group of Israelites who remain faithful to God despite the majority of Israelites rejecting Christ. This idea of a faithful remnant is not unique to Paul and can be found throughout the Old Testament. Paul contends that the remnant is evidence of God's continued faithfulness to His promises to Israel. He also argues that the remnant is proof that God has not rejected Israel but that there is a temporary hardening in part until the full number of Gentiles has come in. The remnant concept is significant because it emphasizes

---

[1] For an extended list, see chapter 6 in "Rabbinic Judaism Debunked: Debunking the myth of Rabbinic Oral Law."

God's faithfulness and ultimate plan for Israel.

To provide evidence for the existence of a remnant, I present a non-exhaustive list of notable Jewish figures throughout history who have professed their belief in Jesus within various Christian denominations. It took a lot of research to find some of them:

1. Pope Evaristus (1st century) - Born to a Hellenistic Jewish family in Bethlehem, he is considered a martyr according to Catholic tradition.
2. Joseph of Tiberias (285-356) was an accomplished historian, writer, politician, and public figure in ancient Tiberias.
3. Jacob of Kefar Sakhnia (2nd-3rd century) was a Jewish disciple of Jesus who could supernaturally heal snakebites (Tosefta, Tractate Chulin 2:6).
4. Epiphanius of Salamis (310-402) was born into a family of Romaniote Jews in Beit Govrin. He was a theologian and was considered a saint in both the Orthodox and Catholic churches.
5. Hillel II (4th century) was the president of the Sanhedrin in the fifth generation of the Amorites of Eretz Israel. He was a Hebrew board fixer who secretly believed in Jesus. He confessed his faith to his students before his death, and his baptism is even described by the doctor from Beit Govrin, Epiphanius of Salamis (in his book "Penarion").
6. Pietro Pierloni ben Baruch Leoni Anacletus II (12th century) was a wise Jew who became an "anti-pope."
7. Gregorios Bar Hebraeus (1226-1286) was a learned doctor, member of a family of doctors, philosopher, theologian, and historian. His writings are still a central point in the study of the history of Judaism in Islamic countries.
8. Abner of Burgos (1270-1347) was a physician, philosopher, and apologist who authored "Mora Tzedek" and came to faith in Jesus as a result of a dream.
9. Rabbi Shlomo Halevi (1351-1445) was a Rabbi and the most influential Jew in Burgos. He became an archbishop for years, and his writings were praised by Rabbi Yitzchak Bar Shesht Barfat (Sage).
10. Rabbi Alfonso de Alcala (15th century) was a Rabbi, doctor, and professor of medicine who translated the Bible into Latin.
11. Alfonso de Zamora (1474-1544) was a Jewish sage, Rabbi,

professor of Hebrew at the University of Salamanca, and editor of the Hebrew text of the Complotonian Polygot.
12. Rabbi Pablo de Coronel (1480-1534) was a Rabbi and professor of Hebrew at the University of Salamanca.
13. Immanuel Tremellius (1510-1580) was a Professor of Hebrew at the prestigious Cambridge University.
14. Jacob ben Haim Ibn Adonijah (1470-1538) was a researcher of Bible translations into Aramaic, an expert on the wording of the Masora, and publisher of 'Great Scriptures.'
15. Rabbi Shmuel Viyoas of Jerusalem (16th century) was the author of the 'Refining Book' procedure, which stopped the burning of Jewish books.
16. Moshe ben Aharon (1716-1670) was a Hazlitt Hebrew teacher at Uppsala University.
17. Yehuda Yona Hatfati (17th century) was an author and translator of the Hebrew language for the Vatican.
18. Professor David Mendel (1789-1850) was a theologian and historian.
19. Dr. Benjamin Disraeli (1804-1881) was a Prime Minister of England.
20. Theodor Kohn (1845–1915) was the seventh Archbishop of Olomouc. In 1904 he was forced to resign due to his Jewish origin.
21. Shalom Ash (1880-1957) was a famous writer and playwright in the Yiddish language.
22. Rabbi Yitzhak Lichtenstein (1824-1909) served as chief rabbi in Hungary.
23. Shmuel Yitzchak Yosef Shershebsky (1831-1906) was the founder of a university in China and a translator of the Bible into the Chinese language.
24. Rabbi Chil Salustovsky (20th century) served as Secretary of the Chief Rabbinate in Jerusalem.

Today, we see an increasing interest in Jesus' teachings among Jewish individuals. However, once they are willing to learn more, they often find themselves disillusioned by certain doctrines that some Christians incorporate while presenting the Gospel to them. This can often result in these Jews retreating from their initial eagerness to learn more about Jesus (a topic I'll explore in reason number three).

Jewish Theological Objections to Jesus

My 2019 book, "Refuting Rabbinic Objections to Christianity," addressed Judaism's most common objections to Christianity. Therefore, I will only briefly address Judaism's two most significant objections to Christ in this book. The first objection concerns the triune God and the divinity of Christ, while the second is the claim that Jesus failed to bring about world peace.

The Trinity and Christ's Divinity

Judaism is a strictly monotheistic faith that emphasizes the oneness and indivisibility of God. Jewish theology maintains that God is unique, incomparable, and indivisible. According to Judaism, God is transcendent (existing beyond time and space) and immanent (present within His creation), yet He has no parts or personalities. This understanding differs significantly from the concept of a triune God in Christianity, where God is depicted as one God who eternally exists as three distinct Persons.

In Judaism, the unity of God is a fundamental tenet that distinguishes it from other religions, particularly polytheistic ones. The belief in the oneness of God is essential to the Jewish faith, and this concept is rooted in the teachings of the Bible and the Talmud. Jewish people often point Christians to verses such as Deuteronomy 6:4: "Hear, O Israel! The Lord is our God, the Lord is one!"

The unity of God in Judaism has several significant implications for understanding the nature of God.

One important aspect is that God's attributes and actions are understood to be part of His one unified being rather than distinct persons or entities. For instance, in Jewish thought, God is both just and merciful, encompassing both qualities in a unified existence. This belief has shaped the course of Jewish history, rituals, and ethics, reinforcing that there is only one God to whom all worship and allegiance is due.

Some portrayals of the Godhead by Christian fundamentalists often reveal an apparent dichotomy, where the Father is depicted as angry, hateful, wrathful, and judgmental, while the Son is painted as gentle, kind, and loving. This perception may suggest a lack of unity within the Godhead.

In contrast, the emphasis on God's oneness in Judaism stresses the concept of a single-minded deity. This starkly contrasts the interpretations of some Christian fundamentalist preachers, who depict God as if he possesses conflicting personality traits, akin to a split personality or bipolar disorder, which implies an internal conflict within the Trinity.

Again, the Father is portrayed as harsh, angry, and legalistic, while the Son is forgiving, gentle, and merciful. As if the Father represents a merciless rigid judge seeking cruel punishment, while the Son represents a compassionate arbiter looking to peacefully resolve any conflict. Some popular descriptions suggest that the Son's sole purpose was to save us from the Father by allowing the Father to abuse and torture him so he may be appeased and spare us.

Allow me to share a couple of examples.

Nick Batzig, a senior pastor and writer for the popular Calvinistic-fundamentalist websites "The Gospel Coalition" and "Ligonier Ministries" with several million followers online, wrote:

> *Is it right, in any sense whatsoever, to say that the Father was angry with the Son when He punished the Son in our place...He made the Son the object of His just displeasure and anger...*[76]

Another example is from the founder of Mars Hill Mega Church, reformed-Baptist pastor Mark Driscoll:

> *See, at the cross of Jesus, there is hatred for Jesus and love for us...*[77]

Likewise, reformed-Baptist pastor and member of "The Gospel Coalition," Thabiti Anyabwile, explains that:

> *Spiritual wrath from the Father occurs deep down in the very godhead itself...something was torn in the very fabric of the relationship between Father and Son...the ancient, eternal fellowship between Father and Son was broken as divine wrath rained down like a million Soddoms and Gomorrah's."*[78]

And the last example, a Christian magazine wrote, "God tortured His son and Himself to release the bondage and grip of sin on His creation."[79]

To the Jewish mind, these descriptions of God sound foreign, pagan, unacceptable, and blasphemous. The concept of God in Judaism is fundamentally different. The Jewish faith emphasizes that all of God's attributes and actions are part of a single, unified being, unable to detach from Himself, hate itself, or be angry with Himself. This belief distinguishes Judaism from other religious traditions and shapes its core teachings and practices.

As a Jew, I always felt uncomfortable with some of the fundamentalist Christians who portrayed God in this way to Jewish friends of mine, having to undo and reexplain my own views later.[II]

The doctrine of the Trinity is arguably the most challenging Christian concept for Jews to comprehend. It can often appear as if Christians are endeavoring to articulate a concept that, by its nature, may exceed human understanding or perhaps even be beyond what is intended for full human comprehension. I have read books, taken seminary courses, watched debates on the doctrine of the Trinity, and even spent many hours trying to convey the idea to my Jewish friends. However, if we are honest with ourselves, we must acknowledge that while the church fathers did their best to describe what they believed God is like, the concept remains vague and debatable, with most attempts to illustrate the Trinity through analogies being all the more confusing (For example, you must have heard before how the Trinity is like water in three different forms: liquid, ice, and vapor. This, however, describes Modalism, not Trinitarianism.)

Many Christians view the Nicene Creed as determining Christian theology just as much as the Bible. While I appreciate and respect what the church fathers had to contribute, I don't believe their views were divinely inspired, perfect, and without error. Plus, we know that some early Church Fathers tried to reconcile Christian thought with Greek philosophy in their theology, while few others were anti-Semitic and rejected anything that sounded Jewish and, in some

---

[II] In fact, In early 2023, I published a book precisely on that: "The "Gospel" of Divine Abuse: Redeeming the Gospel from Gruesome Popular Preaching of an Abusive and Violent God."

cases, gave little to no weight even to the Hebrew Scriptures.

But as another Jewish-Christian scholar friend said, "They got it as close as you can in the Greek language," referring to their attempt to explain the nature of the triune God.

Our human brains may be ill-equipped to fully comprehend the nature of God. Or, as another friend and professor of theology at DTS stated, "If we could really figure God out, we wouldn't be able to worship Him." I concur with that statement. While I find Trinitarianism to be the most compelling explanation of the Godhead, I can also appreciate various other attempts to explain God (such as Modalism and Unitarianism) and have friends with differing beliefs, all of whom I consider sincere in their faith. So as you can tell, I am not as dogmatic about this issue as some fundamentalists might be.[III]

In this discussion, however, I will attempt to demonstrate that the concepts of both the Trinity and the Divinity of Christ, as complex and complicated as they are, may not be as foreign to Judaism as they initially appear.

The Jewish Trinity

While Christianity posits that Jesus is the divine Son of God and a part of the Holy Trinity - consisting of the Father, Son, and Holy Spirit - Judaism firmly upholds the belief in a singular, indivisible God. This fundamental difference creates a theological divide between the two faiths, as the notion of God taking human form and the idea of a triune deity directly contradict the principle of monotheism held by *modern* Judaism. Consequently, the doctrines of Christ's divinity and the Trinity are significant stumbling blocks in the theological dialogue and understanding between Christians and Jews.

But in fact, just like some Christians, Jews often misunderstand the Christian concept of the Trinity. For instance, thinking that Christians believe in a group of three separate gods rather than one,

---

[III] This might be due to my Jewishness. In Judaism, there is often an acceptance of diverse beliefs or doctrines, allowing for the possibility that one's understanding may not be entirely set in stone and open to multiple perspectives. In contrast, Christianity, especially in its fundamentalist version, can sometimes seem more dogmatic, requiring individuals to pledge allegiance to a particular view while outright rejecting alternative perspectives. Considering that the Bible itself never uses the word "Trinity" nor it offers a systematic teaching of God's nature, it's hard for me to be dogmatic about it myself, but respect those who do.

as worded by rabbi Daniel Ballas:

> *According to the Christian belief, the creator of the universe is three gods, whom they call the 'Holy Trinity.' The 'Trinity' is the name given to their group of gods.*[80]

Evidently, the notion of the New Testament teaching a belief in three gods or a group of gods is either a misunderstanding or a straw man argument. In fact, the New Testament consistently teaches that God is one:

> **One** *God and Father of all, who is over all and through all and in all (Ephesians 4:6)*

> *We know that "An idol is nothing at all in the world" and that "There is no God but **one**." (1 Corinthians 8:4)*

Of course, the term "Trinity" is not found in the Bible. Instead, it is a traditional name for a theo/logical argument seeking to best explain the nature of a God who is three persons in one essence. This can also be argued from the Torah itself.

The Hebrew Bible opens up with the first two verses of Genesis, revealing the Creator as more than one distinct person or manifestation; "God" and "the Spirit of God." Genesis 1:1-2 states,

> *In the beginning, **God** created the heavens and the earth. Now the earth was formless and empty, darkness was over the surface of the deep, and the **Spirit of God** was hovering over the waters.*

A few verses later, it is written:

> *Then God said, "Let **us** make mankind in **our** image, in our likeness." (Genesis 1:26).*

In this instance, we read about God and the Spirit of God, and then God refers to himself in the plural. Despite Judaism's belief,[IV] it is not likely that God counseled with the angels — or anyone else — during the creation process of mankind, as evident in Isaiah 44:24 and Nehemiah 9:6.

Other books in the Bible, such as the Psalms, Proverbs, Isaiah, and Daniel, describe a third figure, "the Son," in addition to God and the Spirit of God. In the book of Isaiah, for example, God refers to the Messiah as His child and son, attributing His own divine attributes to the Messiah:

> *For to us a child is born, to us a son is given, and the government will be on his shoulders. And he will be called Wonderful Counselor, Mighty God, Everlasting Father, Prince of Peace. Of the greatness of his government and peace there will be no end. He will reign on David's throne and over his kingdom, establishing and upholding it with justice and righteousness from that time on and forever. The zeal of the Lord Almighty will accomplish this.*
> *(Isaiah 9:6-7)*

This child is no ordinary one, for he is not only destined to inherit David's throne, signifying his lineage as the Messiah son of David, but he also embodies the divine titles, such as "Mighty God, Everlasting Father," reserved solely for God. Jewish sages have also interpreted this passage as a prophecy foretelling the divine nature of God's Messiah.

Prof. Ruth Kaniel, a Jewish scholar with a doctorate in Kabbalah and Jewish mysticism, discusses the concept of the Messiah in ancient Judaism. According to her research, the belief in a divine Messiah is not at all foreign to ancient Jewish thought, and various ancient Jewish sources point to a figure that is God-like:

> *The 'Messiah' was regarded as the 'Son of God,' a notion subtly alluded to in the Bible, the*

[IV] According to Rashi's commentary on Genesis 1:26, God created man "in 'our' image" (plural form) to signify that God consulted with the angels: "Since man was in the image of the angels and they would [hence] be jealous of him, therefore He took counsel with them."

> *accounts of the prophets, and the Book of Psalms.*[81]

Even beyond the Bible, ancient pre-Christ Jewish writings demonstrate that at least some in ancient Judaism believed that the Messiah would be the Son of God. For example, in the Dead Sea Scrolls, document 4Q246, known as the "Son of God Scroll, " dating back to the third century BCE, the Jewish expectation for the Messiah is described. This particular scroll interprets Daniel 7:13, asserting that the Messiah to come would be the 'Son of God.'

Many might be surprised to learn that the concept of the Trinity is not entirely alien, even to rabbinic Judaism, albeit under a different name: "Razei Deshlosha" or "The Secret of Three." For example, rabbi Tzvi Nassi explains that in the book of Zohar (Jewish mysticism):

> *The same Holy and Ancient One is revealed in three heads that are included in one head, and he is the head that is exalted three times. The Holy Ancient One is described as three, and even the other lights that are exalted from its source are included in the three.*[82]

This statement, which could easily be mistaken for a Christian quote, is, in fact, a quintessential Jewish thought about the God who manifests himself in three distinct ways.

Yet, the most compelling revelation comes from a prominent Jewish scholar, Prof. Benjamin Sommer (Jewish Theological Seminary), who openly acknowledges that the Trinity is very Jewish. Below are a few quotes from his book "The Bodies of God":

> *For all the trouble that Jewish and Muslim philosophers have had with this notion, the trinity emerges as a fairly typical example of the fragmentation of a single deity into seemingly distinct manifestations that do not quite undermine that deity's coherence. It is appropriate, then, that Christian biblical commentators connect the trinity with Genesis*

> *18, the story of the three visitors who came to Abraham's tent, because that passage presents a banner example of the fluidity of Yhwh's selfhood (p. 132).*
>
> *Classic language of trinitarian theology, such as μια οὐσία, τρεῖς ὑπόστασις [sic] (one nature, three persons, or one substance, three manifestations), applies perfectly well to examples of Yhwh's fluidity in the Hebrew Bible and to the fluidity traditions in Canaan and Mesopotamia (p. 133).*
>
> *The presence of God and of God-as-Jesus on earth is nothing more than a particular form of this old idea of multiple embodiment, and hence no more offensive to a monotheistic theology than J and E sections of the Pentateuch (p. 133).*
>
> *Some Jews regard Christianity's claim to be a monotheistic religion with grave suspicion, both because of the doctrine of the trinity (how can three equal one?) and because of Christianity's core belief that God took bodily form. What I have attempted to point out here is that biblical Israel knew very similar doctrines, and these doctrines did not disappear from Judaism after the biblical period. (p. 135).*

To conclude, Judaism has long recognized God, the Spirit of God, and the Son of God as persons or manifestations through which the one God reveals himself. The Trinity was and is one of the explanations theologians came up with when reading scriptures. This, apparently, includes at least some Jewish theologians as well.

The Jew who became God

A rabbi goes to see his Catholic friend, a bishop. "Listen," says the rabbi, "There's something I've never quite understood about the Catholic church. It's hierarchical, right?"

"True!" says the bishop.

"So," says the rabbi, "if you do a fantastic job as a bishop, you might become...what?"

"Well," says the bishop, "if I'm fortunate, I might become an archbishop!"

"And if you do a great job as an archbishop?" asks the rabbi.

"I suppose I could even become a cardinal someday!" answers the bishop.

"And if you do an outstanding job as a cardinal?" asks the rabbi.

Starting to get slightly annoyed, the Bishop answered, "I guess after that, I could, theoretically, become the Pope."

"And if you do a really great job as the Pope? Then what?" asked the rabbi again.

The upset bishop answered, "What would you expect me to become after the Pope?! God Himself?!"

The rabbi shrugs. "Well, one of our boys made it!"

Jokes aside, the argument that Christianity advocates for the idolatrous idea of a human being evolving into a god is, unfortunately, a misrepresentation. For example, Rabbi Shlomo Aviner states: "Turning a person into a god - by what name shall we call it if not idolatry?"[83]

First, let's acknowledge that we all concur - the pagan notion of a human being evolving into a god is unmistakably idolatrous! However, this argument stems from a misunderstanding of Christian beliefs and constitutes a "straw man argument." The New Testament never taught that a human became God. On the contrary, the New Testament presents Jewish theology at its finest and a self-evident concept to Jews until about a thousand years ago. It asserts that the Messiah is the ultimate embodiment of God in human form.

We witness the fathers, prophets, and kings longing for God to reveal and manifest himself throughout the Bible. This hope is fulfilled in Christ. In Jesus, God approaches us, demonstrating that he is not a cold, distant, or unapproachable deity but one who loves His creation and seeks to reveal himself to it just as any loving parent would. In other words, God is not a theoretical concept on paper, far removed and disconnected from humanity. Instead, he is a God of love who desires to reveal himself to his children, to be close and accessible, and to live and walk among us, just like he once did with Adam and Eve in the garden of Eden (Genesis 3:8). This idea, as prophesied in the Hebrew Scriptures and fulfilled in the New Testament, was actualized in the person Jesus – the pinnacle of God's revelation to humanity.

Now, if you are a Jewish reader and the notion of "God revealing himself to mankind through the Messiah" seems unfamiliar to you or if you suspect that it is not an authentically Jewish concept, consider what Rabbi Abba Bar-Kahana, an Amora (great sage) and a priest who lived before the Talmud was completed, wrote:

> *What is the name of the messianic king? Rabbi Abba bar Kahana said: The Lord is his name, as it is stated: "This is his name that they will call him: The Lord is our righteousness" (Jeremiah 23:6).*[84]

A more modern example comes from Jewish Prof. Ora Limor, who discusses the perception of the divine Messiah in Judaism in the early Middle Ages:

> *During the days of Isidore of Seville, the beginning of the seventh century,...the Jews largely gave up the view that the Messiah would be God himself...here, too, the polemic [against Christianity] can be asserted outwardly as shaping attitudes inwardly. The current [in Judaism] who believed in the divinity of the Messiah was pushed aside, or at least spoke in a softer language, even if did not disappear completely, while the current that saw in the Messiah only a king of flesh and blood prevailed.*[85]

Likewise, Daniel Boyarin, a Jewish Professor of Talmud at UC Berkeley, explains:

> *Many Jews believed that redemption was going to be effected by a human being, an actual hidden scion of the house of David—an*

> *Anastasia—who at a certain point would take up the scepter and the sword, defeat Israel's enemies, and return her to her former glory. Others believed that the redemption was going to be effected by that same second divine figure mentioned above and not a human being at all. And still others believed that these two were one and the same, that the Messiah of David would be the divine Redeemer.*[86]

> *Many Israelites at the time of Jesus were expecting a Messiah who would be divine and come to earth in the form of a human. Thus the basic underlying thoughts from which both the Trinity and the incarnation grew are there in the very world into which Jesus was born and in which he was first written about in the Gospels of Mark and John.*[87]

To conclude, Jewish scholars acknowledge that ancient Judaism once believed that the Messiah would be some sort of an incarnation of God. However, during the Middle Ages, the rabbis, in opposition to the biblical prophets, decided to make a theological U-turn to distance Jewish theology as far as possible from anything resembling "Christian" theology. This shift, however, stands in stark contrast to ancient biblical Judaism, which did indeed teach and believe in the divinity of their Messiah!

Where is the World Peace?

> *If Jesus were the Messiah, you would know it from reading the newspaper because the front page, instead of being about wars, would be about peace. But since Jesus' time until today, more than one hundred and twenty million people have died in wars. (Rabbi Tovia Singer)*[88]

Likewise, Rabbi Yossi Mizrachi claimed that Jesus couldn't be the Messiah because when the true Messiah finally arrives, there will be no more war in the world but global peace.[89]

However, authentic peace emanates from the depths of our souls, and we won't have that peace unless we know we have peace with God. The discord between humanity and God is precisely the issue Christ sought to reconcile. This underscores that the lack of peace is not just an external issue. Even if the warrior Messiah figure of rabbinic Judaism appears and eliminates all of Israel's enemies, we still won't have real peace. It's a misapprehension to assume that eradicating all tanks, missiles, guns, and weapons would naturally engender peace and fraternity. This viewpoint is flawed, as expressions of hatred can take other forms. Harsh words and curses can inflict profound emotional damage, humiliation can leave lasting psychological scars, and constant harassment can slowly erode our sense of self, leading, in many cases, to suicide. These internal conflicts can sometimes inflict a much slower and more agonizing trauma than a physical weapon. Moreover, even if all weapons were to disappear today, people would inevitably find new methods to harm each other, resorting to rudimentary tools like sticks and stones.

The rabbinic concept of a warrior-Messiah assumes that eliminating the bad guys would resolve everything and create harmony. Unfortunately, some circles within fundamentalist-evangelical Christianity adopted this idea as well, believing that Jesus is coming back to renounce the Sermon on the Mount and kill billions of people, forgetting he once taught, "Blessed are the peacemakers." (Matthew 5:9, see also Hebrews 12:14; Romans 12:18; Ephesians 6:15; Galatians 5:22).

However, the notion that destroying anyone who doesn't share your beliefs would make the world a better place is logically and theologically flawed. First, you only have to look at Christian history, whereby millions of Christians killed one another in the Wars of Religion.[V] Or you can look at how Christians often treat one another today. As a Christian friend and leader of an international Christian ministry once told me, "We are the only army in the world that shoots its own soldiers."

I don't believe that killing even more people will bring global peace. True peace can only be achieved by following the example set

---

[V] The wars of religion were a series of wars waged in Europe during the 16th, 17th and early 18th centuries between Catholics and Protestants.

by Jesus in his teachings, life, and death: to relinquish our ego, make sacrifices for those in need, and love even those who do not reciprocate our love. We make peace with them by loving our enemies (Matthew 5:44), not killing them.

I am not at all a pacifist, and I know very well that war is sometimes unavoidable. I also believe that soldiers, police officers, courts, and prisons exist for a reason. My point is, however, that the Messiah's peace will not come through killing billions of people. Such a notion is self-contradictory, in my view.

Two Messiah[VI]

Ancient Jewish teachings posited various interpretations of who the Messiah would be. Some rabbis taught there are two primary roles for the Messiah. Firstly, the Messiah was envisioned as sacrificing himself, suffering, and dying to atone for our sins. Secondly, he was seen as a ruler tasked with establishing peace and order. Over time, Jewish sages debated whether the Messiah would arrive as a humble, suffering servant riding on a donkey or as a celestial warrior king. Some rabbis even proposed a blend of these interpretations - a messiah on a flying donkey (not joking!). In Sanhedrin 98a, the Talmud explores various notions of the Messiah's arrival, referring to Zechariah 9:9. The text suggests that if the people of Israel are virtuous, the Messiah will make a miraculous entrance from the heavens, riding on a donkey capable of flight.

In these discussions, other Jewish commentators theorized about two distinct messiahs: the "Messiah son of Joseph," who, like the biblical Joseph, would face rejection by his brethren and be presumed dead, and the "Messiah son of David," who would co-reign with the resurrected Messiah son of Joseph.

However, the Christian view is that the Bible mentions only one Messiah, envisioned in two distinct roles at different points in time. Initially, the Messiah is prophesied to be rejected, to suffer, and to die for humanity (for reasons that include atoning for our sins[VII]), only to be resurrected thereafter. The second role anticipates the Messiah's

---

[VI] Based on my book, "Refuting Rabbinic Objections to Christianity."
[VII] I offer an extended discussion on historical theories regarding why Jesus died, beyond atoning for our sins, in my book "The 'Gospel' of Divine Abuse." I believe every Christian must be familiarized with these theories as they give a greater understanding of Christ's work on the cross, including its Jewish background.

return at the end of the days to establish global peace, but not before humanity has learned certain crucial lessons.

The path to peace that Christ proposes begins with resolving the discord between humanity and God. Jesus' sacrifice serves to mend this relationship, enabling us to draw closer to God and thereby experience inner peace. However, Christ did not die to change God's mind about us but to change our minds about God. Instead of an angry, hateful god like the gods of the pagans surrounding Israel, Christ introduced a loving Father willing to give up everything for the sake of his loved creation. This simple acknowledgment of who God truly is can bring peace to even the most bitter, hateful heart. Once bitterness and hate are gone, this internal tranquility can ripple outwards, fostering peace with fellow humans, even those perceived as enemies. The Messiah's role in ushering in peace isn't about eliminating adversaries or attaining superficial peace by means of fear. Instead, it involves forging genuine peace by first addressing the divide between humanity and God. Peace with God is what Jesus achieved during his first advent, allowing us to reconnect with God. Following Jesus' example and teachings, we, too, can contribute to the Kingdom of Heaven (Romans 14:17).

REASON #2: WHAT WAS DONE TO US IN JESUS'S NAME

CHRISTIAN ANTISEMITISM & REPLACEMENT THEOLOGY

Replacement Theology

*Christianity argues that God was fed up with
Israel, revoked his covenant and replaced Israel
with Christianity...Christians teach that God
broke his covenant with Israel.
(Rabbi Moshe Rat)[90]*

Have you ever strolled through a museum admiring paintings only to notice that Jesus and his disciples are depicted with distinctly European features? Their complexions are fair, their noses delicate, and their hair often light in color. These prominent Jewish figures from Israel appear far from authentically Jewish or Israeli in these artistic representations. The Jewish-Israeli Messiah, Yeshua, has been replaced with a gentile, Europeanized Jesus. This alteration skews our perception of these historical figures. It symbolizes the cultural and theological shift in the church regarding Israel.

For nearly two millennia, most of the Christian Church, including Orthodox and Protestant denominations, has maintained that the Jewish people's rejection of Jesus as their Messiah resulted in God's rejection of Israel. Consequently, not only their nation and temple were destroyed, but it is believed that God has abandoned them, leaving them without any purpose regardless of His promises and covenants. Essentially, due to their rebellion against God by rejecting Jesus, it is taught that God replaced Israel with the Church, transferring the blessings (but not the curses) initially promised to Israel to the Church instead. This idea originated with the church fathers.

Origen of Alexandria (185-254 AD), one of the earliest theologians, considered by some to be "the greatest genius the early church ever produced,"[91] proclaimed that the Jews were to blame for killing Jesus.[92]

However, the belief that the Jews are solely responsible for the death of Jesus is refuted by Acts 4:27, which identifies a conspiracy involving Herod, Pontius Pilate, Gentiles, and Jews. Furthermore, all people are accountable for Jesus' death as we have all sinned (Romans 3:23). Christ died for all sinners (1 Corinthians 15:3). Even theologically speaking, blaming only the Jewish people for Christ's death —which needed to happen for our own sake— is to miss the point.

From the subsequent step, 'the Jews killed Christ,' the next logical step would be 'God hates the Jews and has revoked His promises to them. For example, Eusebius (3rd century), a bishop and scholar of the biblical canon who is regarded as one of the most important Christians during late antiquity,[93] taught that the blessings promised to Israel in Scripture were meant for the church. In contrast, the curses were meant for the Jews alone. He also asserted that because the Jews rejected Christ, the Church was the "true" Israel.[94]

This concept, known as "Replacement Theology," is embraced by the majority of professing Christians today. As a result, they view modern-day Israel as a mere historical coincidence devoid of any spiritual significance and the Jews as a group that somehow was lucky enough to survive for an extremely long time and against all odds. These individuals believe God no longer has plans for the Jewish people, considering the regathering of the Jews and the re-establishment of the state of Israel as merely historical accidents with no spiritual importance.

In "Dialogue with Trypho the Jew," one of the earliest known dialogues between Christianity and Judaism from the 2nd century AD, the assertion first appears that the church replaced Israel. A church father, Justin Martyr (100–165 AD), wrote: "We, who were carved out of the bowels of Christ, are the true race of Israel."[95] The discourse surrounding replacement theology expanded as these debates intensified during the Middle Ages. Several rabbinic commentaries from the end of the first millennium AD[96] reflected this Christian theological perspective.

According to Professor Michael Avi-Yona:

> *The sages mockingly rejected the Christians' assertion that they were the true Israel. In opposition to the written Torah, which Christians claimed for themselves, the sages highlighted the Oral Torah's reality, which excluded Gentiles. The sages also alluded to divisions among Christian sects, contrasting them with the unity of Judaism. Rabbi Barachia*

> *stated, "This is how the nations of the world are: these say, 'We are Israel, for us the world was created,' and these say, 'We are Israel,' etc."[97]*

Replacement Theology is the theological basis which fueled the abhorrent rise of anti-Semitism against Jews. In the past century, numerous studies and books have established a link between replacement theology and Christian anti-Semitism.[98,99,100]

As the Middle Ages drew to a close, the situation escalated due to the rise of medieval art, particularly paintings of Biblical narratives. In these artworks, Jewish individuals were often portrayed as sinister figures in league with the devil, collectively scheming to execute Christ. This characterization branded them as "Christ killers," further perpetuating antisemitic stereotypes.

How does a Christian explain Israel?

For 2,000 years, the concept of Israel has perplexed many within the Church. Lacking a language and land, a nation is left without a clear path forward, and historically speaking, such people groups disappear within a few generations. Consequently, the question of Israel's fate has remained contentious, with various theological perspectives emerging over time.

Despite this uncertainty, the concept of Israel remains crucial for Christianity. Israel's history and connection to the Jewish people are integral to understanding God's plan for humanity. The Jewish people were chosen by God to bear His message and bring about His plan of salvation, culminating in Jesus being born to Jewish parents in the Land of Israel. However, most Christians have silenced and ignored the question of how this relates to the Church and its role in God's plan.

In the 14th-16th centuries, with the printing press becoming popular and widespread, Christians became unbound by their religious leaders' guidance, now able to investigate biblical texts independently.

As Jews, we owe a great debt of gratitude to the invention of the modern printing press. Consider the impact on a Christian reading the New Testament for the first time in their life and encountering this verse:

> *I ask then: Did God reject his people?*

> *By no means! I am an Israelite myself,*
> *a descendant of Abraham, from the tribe of*
> *Benjamin. God did not reject his people, whom*
> *he foreknew. (Romans 11:1-2)*

A spiritual awakening among Christian believers who recognized that the Bible and New Testament conveyed a different narrative than what they often heard in their churches and from their priests began.

These Christians believed that the Jewish people played a significant role in God's plan for humanity, as "through their fall salvation has come unto the Gentiles" (Romans 11:11). Therefore, Israel was indeed used by God and therefore remains a crucial aspect of God's plan of salvation and will play a significant role in the end times as well. These Christians view the re-establishment of Israel as a nation in 1948, as well as the survival of the Jews, as fulfilling biblical prophecy.

As an Israeli Jewish-Christian, I consent with this view, believing God is not at all done with Israel. In fact, I believe the best is yet to come!

The question of Israel's fate and how it relates to the Church and God's plan for humanity continues to be a source of theological discussion and debate. However, exploring what that looks like is beyond the scope of this book.

Is Replacement Theology Biblical?

One of the main challenges facing Replacement Theology is that it directly contradicts several teachings found in the New Testament itself. One such example is Acts 1:6-7, where Jesus' disciples asked whether He would restore the kingdom to Israel at that time. Jesus did not correct them but answered that it was not for them to know when. While it is true that Christ is present in the hearts of believers, the Bible also teaches that Yeshua will return to establish a physical kingdom.

Much like Acts, in Romans 9-11, Paul puts Israel as the central theme. The covenant God made with Abraham, promising to bless the whole world through his descendants and give them the land of inheritance, is still expected to be fulfilled in the future. The salvation of Israel is national and includes the return to the land from exile, repentance, forgiveness, and the restoration of the kingdom of God the way it ought to be. It is not because Israel will turn perfect, but because "God's gifts and his call are irrevocable." (Romans 11:29)

While Israel may not be at the center of attention at this moment, this is only temporary (Romans 11:25). The rebelliousness of the people of Israel is not a permanent condition, and their salvation is tied to the promises of the New Testament regarding the future restoration of Israel in their land.[VIII] Regardless of what that might look like in reality or if some of it is figuratively speaking, the fact remains that God is not yet done with Israel.

Furthermore, Paul also emphasizes that God has not abandoned His people and points to the fact there is still a remnant of believers within Israel who follow Jesus. In verse 1, Paul poses a question that strikes at the heart of Replacement Theology: **"Did God reject his people?"** In response, he unequivocally states, "*May it never be!*"

Paul's passionate response to the idea of God rejecting Israel highlights the importance of our faith in a God who stands behind his words.

The salvation of the Gentiles is intertwined with the salvation of Israel (Romans 11:25-26), and the fulfillment of the promises made to Israel is a crucial aspect of God's plan for the world.

If God were to change his mind about his promises to Israel, how could anyone trust His promise of salvation? It would be like a child growing up in fear that their parent might disown them and cast them out of the house any day. As children of God, we need to know we can trust God to live up to his promises and not be capricious or indecisive, even when we embarrass him by throwing a tantrum. Safety and security is the most basic need of any human being.[IX] This is how God created us, so it is only logical to expect Him to keep His promises- all of them.

Ethically speaking, Replacement Theology directly contradicts the character of God and the teachings found in the Old and New Testaments. The salvation of Israel remains a central theme

---

[VIII] Regarding the claim that God has already fulfilled the land promises to the Jews during the time of Joshua: Psalm 105:8-11, written by David long after Joshua, declares the everlasting nature of the land promise and its yet-to-be-fulfilled state. The Jews have never fully occupied all the land promised to them in the Abrahamic Covenant (Genesis 15:18-21).

[IX] According to Maslow's Hierarchy Of Needs

throughout the Bible, and the promises made to Israel are still expected to be fulfilled in the future. God is the best coach in the world, and He wants to prove it by winning using the most rebellious, proud, stiffed-neck group in the league; Israel.

Psalm 129:5-8 proclaims that anyone who hates Zion will be put to shame, and believers are cautioned against blessing such individuals.

Two biblical principles need to be emphasized concerning the notion that the Jews have been rejected by God. Firstly, Israel was chosen as God's people to be a witness, not of their perfection but of a relationship between imperfect people and a perfect God (Isaiah 43:10-12). This calling, which is "irrevocable" (Romans 11:29), is meant to show that God loves and works through imperfect people. And that relationship, like any other relationship, includes ups and down.

Secondly, in contradiction to Replacement Theology, the Bible affirms that God has not rejected the Jews due to their unbelief. In Romans 3:1-4, Paul declares that Israel's rejection of Jesus has not invalidated God's faithfulness to His promises:

> *What advantage, then, is there in being a Jew, or what value is there in circumcision? Much in every way! First of all, the Jews have been entrusted with the very words of God. What if some were unfaithful?* **Will their unfaithfulness nullify God's faithfulness? Not at all!** *Let God be true, and every human being a liar. As it is written: "So that you may be proved right when you speak and prevail when you judge."*

In Romans 11:1-2 Paul testifies that he himself is proof God did not forsake Israel because he himself a Jew who follows Jesus:

> *I ask then, did God reject His people? Certainly not!* **I am an Israelite myself, a descendant of Abraham, from the tribe of Benjamin.** *God did not reject His people, whom He foreknew.*

Even if we were to momentarily entertain the idea that God

intended to abandon the people of Israel in favor of the Gentiles, we would encounter a dilemma: Jesus was an Israeli Jew, as were his disciples. Suppose God truly desired to forsake Israel and turn to another group of people. In that case, He should have chosen a Greek, Egyptian, Edomite, Babylonian, Moabite, Assyrian, Ammonite, or another non-Jew, rather than Jesus, a Jew from the tribe of Judah.

While the Jews are currently under discipline for rejecting our own Messiah, our preservation throughout history is an overwhelming testimony to God's promises.

The prophets consistently warned Israel of discipline for unfaithfulness yet always promised preservation, as seen in Jeremiah 30:11:

> *"For I am with you," declares the Lord, "to save you; for I will destroy completely all the nations where I have scattered you, only I will not destroy you completely. But I will chasten you justly, and will by no means leave you unpunished."*

God's love for the Jewish people is evident in Zechariah 2:8, where He proclaims them "the apple of His eye" and warns anyone who would harm them. In Jeremiah 31, God makes a promise stating that the descendants of Israel will never cease to be His people as long as the laws of nature remain in place:

> *This is what the Lord says, he who appoints the sun to shine by day, who decrees the moon and stars to shine by night, who stirs up the sea so that its waves roar—the Lord Almighty is his name: "Only if these decrees vanish from my sight," declares the Lord, "will Israel ever cease being a nation before me."(Jeremiah 31:35-36)*

This promise assures us that God has a plan for the people of Israel and that he never changed his mind about it. The idea that the Church is "plan B" because God failed to work it out with Israel is false. God will not reject His people, no matter how unfaithful they are (2 Timothy 2:13) – just as you will never reject your small child, no matter how bad they behave. The imagery of the heavens and the earth's foundations being explored above underscores the eternal nature of God's promise. In other words, just as the sun, the moon, and the stars still shine in the sky, we can be sure that God has a plan for Israel. His promises to Israel will be fulfilled whether we can see and understand it or not and whether we like it or not.

Debunking Replacement Theology's Arguments

The New Testament is a definite anti-Semitic book with plots against the Jews! (Rabbi Daniel Asor.)[101]

Indeed, Replacement Theology, promoted by many Christians, is largely based on interpretations of different biblical passages *taken out of context*. Mainly: Romans 9:6, Matthew 21:43, Galatians 3:7, 9, Galatians 3:28-29, Galatians 6:16, and Revelation 2:9. Let's quickly survey them.

Matthew 21:43

Therefore I tell you that the kingdom of God will be taken away from you and given to a people who will produce its fruit.

Matthew 21:43 is often cited to suggest that the kingdom of God will be taken from the Jews and given to the Gentiles. However, as theologian Arnold Fruchtenbaum argues,[102] the kingdom will be taken from that generation and given to a future generation of the people of Israel. One possibility is Jesus' Jewish disciples. They and the early Christian community in Acts 2 were mainly composed of Jews, and they are likely the "people who will produce its fruit."

Otherwise, Matthew 23:37-38 describes Jerusalem being judged despite Jesus' attempts to prevent it. Nevertheless, verse 39 offers hope, as Jesus predicts that a day will come when the people of Israel will accept Him as the Messiah. Suppose Jesus did not speak of His Jewish disciples and the first church. In that case, the future generation, the Israel who would finally accept Jesus in the future ('All Israel' who will be saved; Romans 11:26), is the generation Jesus spoke about.

However, even if we insist that the people mentioned in Matthew

21:43 refers to the Church in general, we must not forget that Abraham was promised to be "a great nation" and that he would bless many nations (Genesis 12:2-3). Therefore, including the Gentiles in the kingdom does not replace or exclude the Jewish part of the church, which is the stump onto which the branches were later grafted into.

Galatians 3:7, 9

Understand, then, that those who have faith are children of Abraham...So those who rely on faith are blessed along with Abraham, the man of faith.

I can say that the guy who led me to Christ almost 25 years ago is my "spiritual father" (regardless of us not having any blood connection). Likewise, in Galatians 3, the apostle Paul argues that Abraham is the *spiritual* father of all believers, not that Gentile believers physically become Jews (or replace them).

Galatians 3:28-29

There is neither Jew nor Gentile, neither slave nor free, nor is there male and female, for you are all one in Christ Jesus. If you belong to Christ, then you are Abraham's seed, and heirs according to the promise.

Paul's message in Galatians 3:28-29 may seem to suggest that there is no longer any distinction whatsoever between Jews and Gentiles. However, it is essential to understand that Paul is not advocating for eliminating all differences between people. Instead, he emphasizes that everyone is invited to join God's spiritual family through faith in Christ Jesus, regardless of their origins, status, or gender.

In the Second Temple period of Judaism, the temple was divided into several sections, and access to these sections varied based on one's status and gender.

Paul's message was particularly significant in a society where only Jewish men were allowed to enter some parts of the Temple. Through Christ, this division and enmity between Jews and Gentiles, male and female - has been abolished, and access to God is open to everyone, regardless of their background.

However, it is essential to note that this does not mean all distinctions and roles are eliminated. Paul acknowledges these distinctions' importance in other parts of his writings. For example, he acknowledges that the gospel was intended for the Jews first (Romans 1:16). He also wrote that slaves should obey their masters (Ephesians 6:5). Similarly, he acknowledges that males and females do have distinct roles (Ephesians 5, 1 Timothy 2-3).

Thus, while Paul emphasizes the unity and spiritual equality of all believers in Christ, he also acknowledges the importance of various roles and distinctions within society and the faith community. Just as Paul was not seeking to demolish the uniqueness and differences between males and females, he did not seek to cancel the identity and distinctions of Jews and Gentiles.

Galatians 6:15-16

Neither circumcision nor uncircumcision means anything; what counts is the new creation. Peace and mercy to all who follow this rule— [even] to the Israel of God.

Galatians 6:16 is often translated as suggesting that the church is 'Israel,' replacing the ethnic nation of Israel. However, this interpretation is based on the assumption that the Greek word "Kai" in the passage should be translated as *'even to,'*[103] which is rarely ever used in the New Testament.[104] The more common interpretation is *"in addition," "and,"* or *"also,"* In Galatians 6:16, Paul is blessing all believers *in addition* to the believing Jews within the church. Paul blesses them for rejecting the false doctrine that the Law of Moses must be kept in order to be saved.

In other words, some translators of the text decided it couldn't possibly mean that Paul intended to bless the house of Israel in addition to the Gentile followers of Yeshua. Consequently, they chose a less common interpretation of the grammar, merging the two groups with no distinction. Although this translation isn't technically incorrect, there are many reasons to adhere to the standard interpretation of the Greek word "καὶ" ("in addition," "and," or "also,"), which is far more common.

"Synagogue of Satan" (Revelation 2:9)

The Jewish and Christian scriptures have long been subject to translation and interpretation. However, the process of translation is not without its challenges and consequences. One significant challenge arises from the linguistic differences between ancient Greek, the original language of the New Testament, and modern English. This issue is particularly evident in translating two ancient Greek words: "Ekklēsia" and " Sunagógé."

Many Christians in modern times are familiar with the term "Ekklēsia," which they often understand to mean "church." However, this interpretation is not entirely accurate. In ancient Greek, "Ekklēsia" and "Sunagógé" were both used to describe gatherings or assemblies.

According to Encyclopedia Britannica:

> The term synagogue is of Greek origin (synagein, "to bring together") and means "a place of assembly."

> Ecclesia, Greek Ekklēsia, ("gathering of those summoned"), in ancient Greece, assembly of citizens in a city-state. Its roots lay in the Homeric agora, the meeting of the people.

In James 2:2, for example, the Greek word "Sunagógé" is translated as "assembly," referring not to a Jewish synagogue but to a Christian church gathering. Therefore, these two words did not carry the modern religious connotations we associate with them today ('Ekklēsia' to mean a Christian church and 'Sunagógé' to mean a Jewish synagogue). Instead, they referred to any type of assembly or gathering, regardless of religious affiliation or context.

Another example is Acts 19:41. In the English Standard Version (ESV) it reads, "he dismissed the assembly." The word for assembly is "Ekklēsia." If "Ekklēsia" indeed meant "church," as commonly believed, the translation should read, "he dismissed the church." However, it wasn't a Christian church at all but a gathering of a "crowd" (verse 35) of random people, most of which "did not even know why they were there" (verse 32).

The inconsistency in translating these words highlights the ideological bias that translators may unknowingly (or knowingly) introduce. The inconsistent translation of these words in the Bible has led to confusion and, in some cases, serious consequences such as antisemitism.

Revelation 2:9 states, "the blasphemy of them which say they are Jews and are not but are the Sunagógé of Satan." Most translations use the term "synagogue" even though the verse specifies that those referred to are not Jews. For the sake of comparison, the New American Bible version translated "the assembly of Satan" (instead of "synagogue"), recognizing its real meaning.

In conclusion, it is clear that the group of individuals attacking the Christians in the City of Smyrna in Revelation 2:9 were not Jews. It is possible that they originated from the Greco-Roman world and were former God-fearers who adopted Jewish customs and practices, similar to some of the Galatians.

Romans 9:6

It is not as though God's word had failed. For not all who are descended from Israel are Israel.

In Romans 9:6, the Apostle Paul specifically addressed the subject of Jewish believers. He introduced the concept of a spiritual remnant within the Jewish people, dubbed 'Spiritual Israel.' This term referred to Jewish followers of Jesus, whom he recognized as the authentic Israel. Consequently, he proposed that the promises designated for the people of Israel were inherited not by all of Jacob's descendants but only by this believing remnant. This group, the real Israel, resembles the remnant of Israel during Elijah's time - those who did not bow to Baal, as Paul reminded his audience in Romans 11:4. The Apostle Paul's perspective, therefore, was that becoming part of the 'true Israel' was not a universal privilege extended to every believer in Jesus Christ but a specific one afforded only to Jewish followers.

The Bible: A Book of Jewish Self-Criticism

Suppose one wishes to find verses that could be taken out of context to establish an anti-Semitic worldview. In that case, they don't have to look solely at the New Testament, as the Hebrew Bible contains instances where the prophets sternly and harshly criticized the religious leaders of the people of Israel. However, it would be inaccurate to label the prophets of Israel as anti-Semitic simply because they chastised their own religious leaders by comparing them to snakes and spiders (Isaiah 59:5). These statements are not considered anti-Semitic, as they were spoken by Jewish prophets, not by a Gentile with malicious intent against the Jewish people.

Likewise, it is inappropriate to claim that Jesus and His disciples, Jews who critiqued the religious leaders of Israel, were anti-Semitic. Just like the prophets Isaiah and Jeremiah did, Jesus, the Prophet of prophets, also criticized the religious leaders of his time with similar epithets ("hypocritical," "snakes," "pythons," "your father the devil," etc.; See Matthew 23).

If the purpose of a prophet is to criticize spiritual leaders, then the role of the Messiah would undoubtedly include similar responsibilities. This is something both Jews and Christians often forget.

During Jesus' time, there was no shortage of criticism directed toward the religious leaders of Israel. This was prevalent even within Judaism itself. Renowned Jewish historian Joseph Ben Mattathias and the Dead Sea Scrolls provide evidence of the corruption and greed that plagued the priesthood and religious leaders of that era. Later, the Talmud itself, in Tractate Pesachim 17, acknowledges and condemns the corruption within the priestly families in Israel during Jesus' time. According to Tractate Yoma 8 and 9, high priests were known to bribe officials. Should we say they, too, were antisemites?

Furthermore, it wasn't just the priesthood that faced accusations of corruption. Prof. David Flusser, a historian from the Hebrew University, details popular opinions among the people of Israel during the Second Temple period regarding the Pharisees, based on the Dead Sea Scrolls, which depict the Pharisees as corrupt and malevolent leaders:

> *The charge of hypocrisy and unrighteousness is levelled by the men of Qumran against the Pharisees. They are also described as swaying the vast majority of Israel of that time. Moreover, according to the pesher Hosea, the people "listened to their deceit, honoured them, and held them in awe as gods."*[105]

Much like any other Jewish writing, the New Testament contains Jewish self-criticism and debates among Jews. Therefore, interpreting these criticisms and arguments out of context can lead to incorrect views of the New Testament as antisemitic by both Jews and Christians, much like misinterpreting arguments between siblings. Family members can speak to one another in ways outsides simple can't.

God Did Not Replace Israel

The New Testament consistently encourages Gentile followers of the Messiah to respect and love the people of Israel, despite their rejection of the Messiah:

> *I have great sorrow and unceasing anguish in my heart. For I could wish that I myself were cursed and cut off from Christ for the sake of my people, those of my own race, the people of Israel. Theirs is the adoption to sonship; theirs the divine glory, the covenants, the receiving of the law, the temple worship, and the promises. Theirs are the patriarchs, and from them is traced the human ancestry of the Messiah, who is God over all, forever praised! Amen.*
> *(Romans 9:2-5)*

In these verses, Paul the Apostle highlights that the Messiah, Jesus, is a Jew, their faith is Jewish, and he himself, as the writer and speaker, is also Jewish.

Through the Jewish Messiah, God established a new covenant, making himself accessible to both Jews and Gentiles. From the outset, God chose the people of Israel to bring the blessing—that is, access to God—to all the nations of the world, all who he created, just as he once promised to Abraham: "…and **all peoples on earth will be blessed through you.**" (Genesis 12:3b) and again, "…and through your offspring, **all nations on earth** will be blessed." (Genesis 26:4b)

The concept of a "New Covenant" (or New Testament) is not a first-century Christian idea; it is fundamentally a Jewish one, rooted in the Hebrew Bible and prophesied by the prophet Jeremiah:

> *"The days are coming," declares the Lord,*
> *"when I will make a **new covenant with the***

> ***people of Israel*** *and with the people of Judah."*
> *(Jeremiah 31:31)*

Jeremiah's prophecy, six hundred years before the New Testament was written, was not about replacing Israel. Establishing a new covenant does not imply that God has replaced His people with a different group. In fact, Jeremiah wrote that the new covenant is "with the people of Israel."

The Sinai Covenant was a collective agreement between God and Israel as a nation. A constitution. Under that covenant, individuals had no direct access to God; only priests could enter the Holy of Holies and communicate with God. In contrast, the new covenant creates a personal relationship between each individual and God. As a result, in the new covenant, access to God is no longer exclusive to priests but available to everyone.

While the first believers to enter that new covenant were almost all Jews, the new covenant also extended an invitation to the rest of humanity—all the Gentiles God created and loves. This covenant welcomes everyone, regardless of their background, to partake in the blessings and promises offered through Yeshua, the Jewish Messiah. This inclusive message aligns with God's intention to share his love, blessings, and redemption with his entire creation.

"First to the Jew" (Romans 1:16)

> *For I am not ashamed of the gospel, because it is the power of God that brings salvation to everyone who believes: **first to the Jew**, then to the Gentile. (Romans 1:16)*

To appreciate the full meaning of Paul's statement that the gospel is "to the Jew first," it is crucial to understand the original Greek word "proton" (πρῶτον). There are two[106] primary ways to interpret this:

The Sequential Interpretation:

The term 'proton' may refer to the chronological order in which the gospel was preached – first to the Jews, then to the Gentiles. However, this view can be misleading, as it may imply that the Jews had their chance in the first century but missed it (while Romans emphasize that God has not forsaken Israel).

The Priority Interpretation:

Alternatively, 'proton' can signify priority, importance, or prominence. In this sense, Paul conveys that the gospel is fundamental to the Jews. This interpretation aligns better with the rest of Romans, portraying the Jewish people as accountable before God due to their prior and unique knowledge and access to divine revelation. Consequently, the gospel holds special significance for the Jews and extends to the Gentiles. Romans chapter 1 teaches that humanity had access to general divine revelation through nature and conscience. Still, the people of Israel had received a special revelation, making them more accountable. Initially, the gospel was incomprehensible to Gentiles since they had no concept of the "Messiah" or the belief in one God.

Conversely, for the Jews, the concept of the Messiah was not only familiar but most eagerly anticipated. The Jewish people are, therefore, particularly (proton) judged as the gospel is especially (proton) relevant for them. However, the gospel is now also and equally for the Gentiles, with the path open to all.

These biblical principles should guide our efforts to fulfill the Great Commission. The church must recognize that the gospel remains particularly and especially significant for the Jewish people, given its historical, contextual, and covenantal connections to Judaism.

"Replacement Theology," which asserts that the church has superseded Israel, is problematic not only because of its arrogance towards Jews but also because it neglects the importance of Romans 1:16 in understanding the Great Commission. The gospel remains as relevant to the Jewish people today as ever. Our task is to joyfully embrace the truth that the gospel is the power of God for salvation, particularly for the Jew and equally for the Gentile.

Romans 11 and Ephesians emphasize that Gentiles, alongside Israel, can be included and grafted into the family of God equally. When sharing the gospel with Jewish people, we are not asking them to abandon their ancestral faith but inviting them to return home.

Due to historical tensions between the Church and Judaism, Jewish people often perceive Christianity as wholly incompatible with their Jewish identity. When invited to contemplate Jesus, they assume they are being asked, once again, to renounce all ties to their Jewish heritage. Unfortunately, even today, some churches expect Jewish people to do so when they embrace Jesus.

However, this expectation contradicts Scripture. The New Testament recounts the experiences of Jewish believers who, even after accepting Jesus as their Messiah, opted to maintain their connection to Jewish practices for various reasons. These individuals continued to visit the temple for prayer and sacrifice (Acts 3:1; Acts 21:26), observe the Sabbath (Acts 17:1), and celebrate Jewish feasts and customs (Acts 20:16; Acts 21:26; 1 Corinthians 5:8). Just as diverse cultures and ethnic groups can embrace their own traditions while believing in Jesus, Jews should be encouraged to do so as well.

The only question is- what kind of gospel message do Christians communicate nowadays with Jews, as millions of dollars are being poured in yearly to promote "Jewish Evangelism," which doesn't seem to work much. But this discussion is reserved for reason number three.

I have never ever heard of replacement theology. But all the arguments against it are well known to me.

The 'Age of the Gentiles'

Antisemitism

> *Through centuries of struggle, Jews across the world have been witnesses not only against the crimes of men, but for faith in God, and God alone. Theirs is a story of defiance in oppression and patience in tribulation – reaching back to the exodus and their exile into the diaspora. That story continued in the founding of the State of Israel. The story continues in the defense of the State of Israel. (George W. Bush)[107]*

Please be aware that the tone of this section may come across as polemical. As a Jewish author, it is challenging to completely detach my emotions from my writing, especially on the topic of antisemitism, as members of my own family have suffered at the hands of professing Christians and in the name of Christ.

I do recognize that not all Christians are alike; however, for clarity's sake, I will often use the term "Christianity," referring specifically to its antisemitic factions and not asking to generalize, as I, too, am also a follower of Christ.

Antisemitism – an overview

Antisemitism, or hostility and discrimination towards Jews, has a long and complex history within Christianity. While Christianity emerged from Judaism and Jesus himself was a Jew, over the centuries, many Christians have harbored deep-seated prejudices against Jews and Judaism. These attitudes have often been fueled by religious and political ideologies and have manifested in various forms, including violence, persecution, and institutionalized discrimination.

One of the earliest and most influential sources of Christian antisemitism was the New Testament, whereby verses were taken out of context. As we covered earlier, some passages in the New Testament, such as the story of the crucifixion itself, have been used to justify persecution and discrimination against Jews. In addition, the early Christian Church fathers, such as John Chrysostom and

Augustine, wrote extensively about the supposed "evil" of the Jews and the alleged responsibility of the Jewish people for the death of Jesus, further contributing to negative attitudes, including severe persecution, within the Christian community towards Jews in general, which led to a reaction from the Jewish side. A vicious circular cycle that fuels itself. However, the distinction was that the Jewish response was in writing, not through violence. Considering Jesus' commands to love and care – even for your enemy, one would expect the Christians to be on the non-violent side.

Over the centuries, these attitudes have manifested in various forceful ways. During the Middle Ages, Jews were frequently violently persecuted by Christians. In many European countries, Jews were forced to live in ghettos, restricted in their occupations, and subjected to numerous legal and social disabilities. In some cases, such as the infamous Spanish Inquisition, Jews were forced to convert to Christianity or face persecution and execution.

Numerous Church Fathers asserted that every Jew was fundamentally and repulsively un-Christian or anti-Christian and that Jews transmitted indelibly evil characteristics to their descendants.

Consequently, the sacrament of Christian baptism could not cleanse the "stench of Jewish unbelief." Associating Jews with heresy, the second-century Christian apologist Justin Martyr argued that God had given Moses' Law to the Jews to restrain the inherently sinful wickedness of the Jews. Augustine maintained that no Jew could ever escape the stigma of their ancestors' denial and murder of Christ.[108] He wrote that the evil of the Jews, "in their parents [in parentibus], led to death."[109] His mentor, Jerome, claimed that all Jews were Judas and innately evil beings who betrayed the Lord for money.[110] John Chrysostom, early church father and the archbishop of Constantinople, dubbed Jews deicides with no opportunity for "atonement, excuse, or defense."[111] Referencing Jeremiah 13:23, "Can the Ethiopian change his skin or the leopard his spots?" in the seventh century, Isidore of Seville declared that the Jews' evil character never changed.[112]

A Byzantine proverb stated, "When a Jew is baptized, it is as if one had baptized an ass."[113] In the following century, John of Damascus wrote that God granted the Jews the Sabbath due to their "absolute propensity for material things."[114]

The widespread belief was that the Jew was inherently evil and that this evil was in his blood. Therefore, converting them to Christ will not be possible.

These early manifestations of Christian racism persisted into the Middle Ages. When in 1130, Anacletus II, great-grandson of a converted Jew, was elected Pope, Bernard of Clairvaux adopted the racist stance that "it is an insult to Christ that the offspring of a Jew has occupied the chair of Peter."[115] Ironically, forgetting Peter himself was a Jew.

These early forms of Christian racism continued into the modern era, further complicating the relationship between Christianity and antisemitism. It is essential to acknowledge that while not all Christians adhered to racist beliefs, these ideas were widely accepted, persisted within the Christian tradition, and contributed to the climate that enabled the Holocaust. The intersection of Christian theology, antisemitism, and racism created a toxic environment that allowed for the vilification and persecution of Jews throughout history.

The Holocaust should never be solely attributed to Christian ideology, but the longstanding tradition of Christian antisemitism played a significant role in the development and execution of this genocide. To understand the full scope of the Holocaust, one must consider the complex interplay of ideological, historical, and social factors that led to the persecution and extermination of millions of Jews. Recognizing the role of Christianity in this context is not an indictment of the faith as a whole but rather a necessary step in understanding the forces that contributed to one of the darkest chapters in human history.

The Jesuit periodical Civiltà Cattolica, backed and supervised by the Vatican, conducted a racist anti-Semitic crusade from the late nineteenth century until at least 1945. In 1880, Father Giuseppe Oreglia penned:

> *The Jews -- eternal insolent children, obstinate, dirty, thieves, liars, ignoramuses, pests and the scourge of those near and far. Oh how wrong and deluded are those who think Judaism is just a religion, like Catholicism, Paganism, Protestantism, and not in fact a race, a people, and a nation! . . . For the Jews are not only Jews*

> *because of their religion . . . they are Jews also and especially because of their race.*

The following year, Oreglia added that driven by the devil, Jews could not become members of another nation or race, "they are born Jews and must remain Jews. Hatred for Christians they imbibed with their mother's milk."[116]

When newly appointed Archbishop Théodore Kohn (Cohen), a Catholic scholar and convert from Judaism, attempted to address a Catholic Congress in 1896, he faced jeers, and the Vatican requested his resignation.[117]

In 1904, French Catholic newspaper claimed that "the Church of Satan is incarnated in the Jewish race." In 1934, a Polish Catholic journal Pro Christo observed that even after seven generations, converted Jews still emitted their "Jew-stench"—a concept related to the association of Jews with the devil, who smelled like feces.[118]

In the early twentieth century, the Churches disavowed racist attitudes toward Jews, presumably because of the Christian sacrament of baptism, but they often acted as if they were evaluating Jews based on their race. Furthermore, many racists, if not most, do not entirely supplant their pseudo-scientific Judeophobia for their Christian anti-Semitism. Instead, they incorporate their racist ideology into their pre-existing religious prejudice against Jews. Traditional religious anti-Semitism has coexisted with racist anti-Semitism for nearly 2,000 years. For two millennia, through sermons, theological writings, laws, art, and literature, Christian anti-Semitism has focused on the Jews' persistent "sins" and "crimes"—their obstinate adherence to their perfidy, their avarice, their treachery, their servitude, and their murderous fury at Christ and Christians. On some occasions, Christian racism resulted in the mass murder of Jews. Crusaders and other medieval Christians frequently massacred Jews, whom they deemed hopelessly unconvertible, without offering the choice of baptism. These murderers, much like John Chrysostom and Martin Luther, regarded Jews as irredeemably Jewish and deserving of annihilation. The National Socialists harbored similar sentiments and, mutatis-mutandis, opted for the same resolution to the "Jewish Problem."

Following their study of American opinion in the 1960s, Charles Glock and Rodney Stark discovered that even during a period of burgeoning ecumenical harmony led by the Catholic Vatican II

Council, approximately half of the Americans interviewed—Catholic and Protestant, lay and clergy alike—believed that the Jews are responsible for their own suffering.

The narrative that the Jewish people deserve the persecution and dispersal they've faced over the last two millennia due to their rejection of Jesus as the Messiah is common among many Christian perspectives. But have we ever wondered what would have occurred if they had accepted Him?

Imagine, if Jesus had been hailed as their king by the Jews, and His crucifixion had been averted, the vital elements of the Christian faith — atonement for sin through the blood of Christ and the resurrection — would not have transpired. In essence, the birth of Christianity as we know it would not have occurred.

These interview respondents were the same individuals who, associating Jews with materialism, criticized them for being avaricious. The researchers concluded that far from being strictly secular, "the core and essence of anti-Semitism rested on Christianity." A staggering 95 percent of Americans derived their secular stereotypes of Jews from the Christian faith.[119]

Other investigations into prejudice and stereotyping suggest that although the human mind possesses an innate tendency to classify, it does not inevitably categorize others based on race or ethnicity. This results from cultural conditioning. For instance, in England from the seventeenth to nineteenth centuries, Jews were stereotyped similarly to how they had been since the era of the Church Fathers or at least the Middle Ages and would continue to be until the Nazi period, as: cursed, Antichrists, avaricious, blasphemers, brutes, cheats, circumcisers, cowards, crucifiers, cutthroats, deicides, desecrators of the Host, devils, dogs, feces, parasites, foul-smelling, bleeding, infidels, lascivious infidels, locusts, usurers, murderers, obstinate, stiff-necked, peddlers, perfidious, poisoners, pigs, proselytizers, ravens, reptiles, ritual murderers, serpents, witches, subverters, traitors, thieves, tricksters, swindlers, unclean beasts, and wolves. A similar pattern emerged in late nineteenth-century France during the Dreyfus Affair.[120]

Christian associations of the term "Jew" with detestable deeds and traits have been integrated into the languages of the West. In the Deutsches Wörterbuch, initiated by the Brothers Grimm in 1838 (and completed in 1960), "Jude" was defined as "Jew: ...of their evil traits—they are offensive and slovenly, greedy and extortionate. [One says] in a whole variety of idioms—dirty as an old Jew; he stinks like a Jew;...to taste like a dead Jew...to practice usury, to cheat, to profiteer, to borrow like a Jew."

The dictionary also highlighted that "Jew" refers to a portion of a pig's spinal column; to "jew" (jüdeln) signifies talking, bargaining, or smelling like a Jew.[121] In the seventeenth century, Littré's French Dictionary defined "Juif" as someone who accrues money through deceit. In colloquial (Brazilian) Portuguese, as in English, all things associated with Christianity are considered good and valuable, but to "jew" (judiar) implies mistreatment, torment, or mockery. "Judeu," or Jew, denotes a malevolent, miserly individual. One saying proclaims, "A Jew, not a Christian, killed my dove, my dove so tame that it would eat out of my hand." "Judiada" alludes to inhuman, barbarous, and cruel behavior. In popular belief, Jews drank human blood and consumed babies. Who would commit such acts? According to scholar Célia Mentlik, "no other than the Antichrist."[122]

The Oxford English Dictionary contains numerous historical examples of the usage of the words "Jew" and "Jewish" in English.[123] Nearly half of the definitions are compound words that convey offensive and repulsive connotations. For example, a "jewbush" is one that induces vomiting and death.

The term "antisemitism" has traditionally been distinguished from "anti-Judaism," "Judaeophobia," or "Judenhaß."[124] "Antisemitism" (Antisemitismus) is a nineteenth-century German neologism that replaced "Jew-hatred" (Judenhaß) in polite discourse, carrying with it undertones of scientific authority, political activity, and racism. In its narrowest conception, antisemitism suggests that it was not the religion of the Jews that incited hostility (anti-Judaism) but rather the biological-race aspects of the Jewish character as manifested in their behavior.

The historical continuity of anti-Jewish ideas and imagery serves as clear evidence that no fundamental difference exists between anti-Judaism and antisemitism. One recent author has outlined a dozen beliefs held by modern antisemites about Jews: (1) conspiracy, (2) intent to conquer the world, (3) desire to harm Christians, (4) immorality, (5) money-grubbing, (6) control of the press, (7) ruination of Christians economically, (8) creation of godless

Communism, (9) murder of Christian children and drinking their blood, (10) destruction of the Christian religion, (11) traitors to their nation, and (12) the need for segregation and curtailing of Jewish rights.[125] All these traits—control of the press and creation of Communism could be subsumed under "conspiracy"—are not modern but stem from the writings of the Church Fathers and the Christian Middle Ages.

Every Christian is responsible for preventing the shedding of "innocent blood" and should love their neighbors as themselves—both first expressed in the Hebrew Scriptures.[x] Shortly after the Holocaust and World War II, German-Christian philosopher Karl Jaspers posited that as witnesses to any crime, we must intervene to avoid incurring the deepest form of "metaphysical guilt."[126] Choosing to remain silent in the face of evil is a form of complicity, though not as morally reprehensible as directly committing the act. The Church Fathers who established the theological framework portraying Jews as history's most deplorable people, the medieval theologians and some popes who expanded and enforced this system, certain American presidents, some British government officials, National Socialists, and Holocaust deniers—all have played varying yet critical roles in perpetuating the evil of antisemitism, culminating in the unparalleled atrocity of the Holocaust. It is vital to recognize that while history cannot be altered, the past must be examined; we need to learn from and remember the injustices committed in God's name and pledge never to let such evil recur—against Jews or anyone else.

As Christians, it is vital to explore the biblical Jewish roots of the faith to gain a deeper understanding of the Scriptures and the culture from which they originated. However, while doing so, we must also be mindful of the anti-Semitic interpretations of many Church Fathers and avoid perpetuating harmful stereotypes and misconceptions about Judaism and Jewish people. By acknowledging the Jewishness of Jesus and the early Church, we can gain a greater appreciation for the shared history and heritage and develop a more nuanced understanding of how both faiths have evolved over time.

Ultimately, it is essential to approach the early Jewish roots of the Christian faith with humility and an open mind and to seek out resources and perspectives that challenge our assumptions and

---

[x] Gen. 4:9 and Deut. 19:10; see also Num. 35:9–31 and Josh. 20:1–9.

broaden our views. In this way, we can build bridges of understanding and mutual respect between Christians and Jews and embrace the richness and diversity of our shared spiritual heritage.

Early Church Antisemitism

So far, I have provided a bird-eye view of Christian antisemitism. Now, I will explore specific examples, names, and events to highlight the pervasiveness of antisemitism and the persecution of Jews by Christians and in the name of Jesus throughout history. I must emphasize—especially to any Jewish readers—that many Christians have shown love and support for the Jewish people, understanding their moral and spiritual responsibility to care for them and not to boast over them, as stated in Romans 11:18.

Church Fathers

During the early years of Christianity, numerous Church Fathers harbored unfavorable opinions of Jews and Judaism. The origins of Replacement Theology and the resulting anti-Semitism can be traced back to the early stages of Christianity, which is especially ironic given that the first Church was initially a predominantly Jewish movement which was established in Judea by Jewish followers of the Jewish Messiah, with its foundational documents authored by Jews. Regrettably, many influential Church Fathers who played significant roles in shaping early Christianity forgot these facts, promoting anti-Semitism instead, thereby tainting the core of the Christian faith:

- o **Ignatius of Antioch (50-117 AD)** taught that those who partake in the celebration of the Passover are partakers with those who killed Jesus.[127]
- o **Justin Martyr (100-106 AD)** claimed God's covenant with Israel was no longer valid and that the church had replaced the Jews.[128]
- o **Irenaeus (130-202 AD)** declared the Jews were disinherited from the grace of God.[129]
- o **Tertullian (155-230 AD)** blamed the Jews for the death of Jesus and argued they had been rejected by God.[130]
- o **Origen (185-254 AD)** was responsible for much anti-Semitism based on his assertion that the Jewish race was responsible for killing Jesus.[131]

- **Eusebius (275-339 AD)** taught that the blessings of Scripture were meant for the church, while the curses were meant for the Jews. He asserted that the Church was the "true Israel."[132]
- **Hilary of Poitiers (291 – 371 AD)** said, "Jews are a perverse people, accursed by God forever."[133]
- **Sylvester I (314-335),** the pope at the time of Nicaea, ordered:

   No priest shall… be friendly or sociable with Jews, nor should anyone take food of drink with the Jews, for if this was decreed by the holy apostles, it is incumbent upon the faithful to obey their command; and the synod shall excommunicate anyone who does not comply with this order.

- **Gregory, bishop of Nyssa (335–395 AD)**, said:

   Jews are slayers of the Lord, murderers of the prophets, enemies and haters of God, adversaries of grace, enemies of their fathers' faith, advocates of the devil, a brood of vipers, slanderers, scoffers, men of darkened minds, the leaven of Pharisees, a congregation of demons, sinners, wicked men, haters of goodness!

- **Ambrose (340-397 AD)** said:

   The Jews are the most worthless of all men. They are lecherous, greedy, rapacious. They are perfidious murderers of Christ. They worship the Devil. Their religion is a sickness. The Jews are the odious assassins of Christ, and for killing God there is no expiation possible, no indulgence or pardon. Christians may never cease vengeance, and the Jew must live in servitude forever.
   God always hated the Jews.
   It is essential that all Christians hate them.[134]

- **John Chrysostom (349-407 AD)** preached a series of sermons against the Jews in which he stated:

  > *The synagogue is worse than a brothel...it is the den of scoundrels and the repair of wild beasts...the temple of demons devoted to idolatrous cults...the refuge of brigands and debauchees, and the cavern of devils. It is a criminal assembly of Jews...a place of meeting for the assassins of Christ... a house worse than a drinking shop...a den of thieves, a house of ill fame, a dwelling of iniquity, the refuge of devils, a gulf and a abyss of perdition...I would say the same things about their souls... As for me, I hate the synagogue...I hate the Jews for the same reason.*

  Chrysostom also denied that Jews could ever receive forgiveness. He claimed it was a Christian duty to hate Jews and that Jews are Satan worshipers. Chrysostom was canonized a saint.[135]

- **Jerome (347-420 AD)** was the second-most voluminous writer after Augustine of Hippo in ancient Latin Christianity. Jerome described the Jews as:

  > *Serpents wearing the image of Judas. Their psalms and prayers are the braying of donkeys... They are incapable of understanding Scripture.*[136]

- **St. Augustine of Hippo (354-430 AD)** is admired for his many writings, primarily by Protestants, especially Calvinists and Lutherans, who consider him one of the theological fathers of pre-Protestant Reformation times. Augustine asserted that the Jews deserved death but were destined to wander the earth humiliated as a witness to the victory of the church over the synagogue.[137]

It is important to note that these views were not universal among all Christian leaders, as few Christian leaders have actively opposed antisemitism and sought to build positive relationships with Jews.

Significant Church Councils

- Synod of Elvira (305 AD in Spain)

The Synod of Elvira was a council of bishops held in the city of Elvira (present-day Íllora) in the Roman province of Baetica. The counsel prohibited Christians from sharing a meal with a Jew, marrying a Jew, blessing a Jew, or observing the Sabbath.[138] These decisions were part of a larger trend in the early Christian church of distancing itself from Judaism.

- First Council of Nicaea (325 AD in Turkey)

Perhaps the most known Council in Christian history, the first Council of Nicea, was a council of Christian bishops held in Nicaea (now Iznik, Turkey) in 325 CE. It was a significant event in the early history of Christianity and had some consequences for the relationship between Christians and Jews. While the Council of Nicea was not primarily focused on issues of antisemitism or the treatment of Jews, it greatly affected it. The Council of Nicea was called by the Roman Emperor Constantine I, who sought to unite the Christian Church and resolve conflicts over Christian doctrine.
  - None of the bishops of Jewish background were allowed to join the council.[139]
  - The Council Changed the celebration of the Resurrection from the Jewish Feast of First Fruits to Easter in an attempt to disassociate it from Jewish feasts.
  - The Council stated: "For it is unbecoming beyond measure that on this holiest of festivals we should follow the customs of the Jews. Henceforth let us have nothing in common with this odious people."[140]
  - A decision was made to replace Passover with Easter, and to replace the Saturday Sabbath with a Sunday Sabbath.[141]

Emperor Constantine said, "Let us then have nothing in common with the detestable Jewish crowd; for we have received from our Savior a different way."[142]

The persecution of the Quartodecimans marked the beginning of a dark era. The term "Quartodeciman" is Latin for "fourteeners," referring to Jews who celebrated Passover on the 14th of Nisan. As time went on, performing circumcision was outlawed, with violations punishable by death. Eventually, Jews were prohibited from holding public office or serving as officers in the military.[143] Later, restrictions were put on where the Jewish people could live, with whom they could do business, and where they could travel.[144]

Middle Ages (5th - 15th centuries)

Books can and were written about antisemitism during these centuries. I will only highlight several events.

During the Middle Ages, two erroneous beliefs became entrenched in Church doctrine:
1. Jews were deemed "Christ killers" and deserved mistreatment accordingly.
2. The Church had replaced Israel, rendering God's future purpose for the Jewish people obsolete.

Throughout this period, self-professed Christians perpetuated myths that fueled popular animosity and fear toward Jews, resulting in their widespread perception as agents of Satan among Christian communities. Passion plays were prevalent during the Middle Ages and served as a tool to cultivate hatred towards Jewish people. In these plays, Jews were portrayed as demonic figures, fully aware that Christ was the Son of God yet choosing to side with the devil. As Christ carried the cross, he was tormented by malevolent, cursing devils with hooked noses, horns, and tails. Such portrayals painted Jews as evil counterparts to Christ's divine nature.[16]

Nevertheless, despite these challenges, Jews also made significant contributions to the cultural, intellectual, and economic life of Europe and the Middle East during this period.

Sisebut's decrees (612-616)

Sisebut, King of the Visigoths, ruled over Hispania and Septimania from 612 until his death. Upon ascending the throne, he mandated the conversion of his Jewish subjects to Christianity.[145]
In response to his decree, which demanded conversion or expulsion, some Jews sought refuge in Gaul or North Africa, while around 90,000 chose to convert. However, many of these conversos secretly retained their Jewish identities. In 616, Sisebut ordered the

punishment of unyielding Jews with a whipping if they continued to resist conversion to Christianity.

The Crusades (11th-12th centuries)

The Crusades, a series of military campaigns initiated by the Catholic Church in the late 11th and 12th centuries, profoundly affected Jewish communities in Europe and the Middle East. Although the primary objective of the Crusades was to reclaim the Holy Land from Muslim control, Jews were also targeted, suffering violence and persecution during this period.

The First Crusade, spanning from 1095 to 1099, was a particularly notorious instance of antisemitism. European Jews were subjected to violence and persecution; many were killed or forced to flee. Jewish communities in the Holy Land also faced severe consequences, with numerous Jews killed or coerced into converting to Christianity. The contemporary chronicler Ibn al-Qalanisi documented:

> *The Jews assembled in their synagogue, and the Franks burned it over their heads.*[146]

As the synagogue burned, the Crusaders marched around it singing "Christ, We Adore Thee."[147] The irony is that when you burn a synagogue, you also burn the Hebrew Scriptures that are inside the synagogue. This symbolizes much of the Christian attitude towards Jews in the past two millennia.

The Crusades were partly fueled by religious zeal and the ambition to propagate Christianity, with Jews perceived as a religious and cultural threat to this objective. Consequently, Jews were often accused of being enemies of Christianity and subjected to various discriminatory practices, such as wearing distinctive clothing or symbols, being barred from certain occupations or areas, and facing violent assaults.

Jews also experienced numerous economic and social constraints during the Crusades. They were frequently prohibited from engaging in specific occupations or professions and often compelled to pay special taxes or fines. In 1096, during the First Crusade, approximately 12,000 Jews were killed in the Rhine Valley alone. This persecution persisted until the Ninth Crusade in 1272. In 1099, Crusaders trapped the Jews of Jerusalem in a synagogue, set it ablaze, and forced those attempting to escape back into the burning building.

In summary, the Crusades had a considerable and enduring impact on the Jewish community, serving as a stark reminder of the perils of religious intolerance and persecution.

The Clifford's Tower Massacre (1190)

The Clifford's Tower Massacre was a mass murder that occurred on March 16, 1190, in York, England. At the time, York was a center of Jewish settlement in England. The massacre took place at Clifford's Tower, a castle and royal treasury that was being used as a refuge for the city's Jewish population. The massacre was precipitated by a blood libel circulated by certain local community members, accusing the Jews of York of committing ritual murders. This false and inflammatory accusation was used to incite violence against the Jewish community. As a result, a mob of angry locals besieged Clifford's Tower, trapping the Jews inside. Faced with the prospect of being lynched by the mob, many of the Jews chose to commit suicide by setting fire to the tower. Around 150 Jews died in the massacre, either by being burned alive or by taking their own lives.

In 1290, the entire Jewish population of England was expelled from the country on The Edict of Expulsion, a royal decree of King Edward I.

Blood Libels (11th-12th centuries)

One of the most popular anti-Jewish myths that gained widespread acceptance was the notion that Jews murdered Christians each year around the time of Passover to get the blood needed to perform satanic rites. This became known as the charge of ritual murder or "blood libel." Another common myth that circulated during these years was that Jews would steal the wafers used in communion and stab them with knives, thus killing Christ once again![148] Christians also falsely claimed Jews use non-Jews' blood—particularly Christian children—in their religious rituals. This unfounded and incendiary allegation has historically incited violence and persecution against Jews while serving as a pretext for discrimination and aggression.

The first documented blood libel case in Europe during the Middle Ages occurred in 1144 with the case of William of Norwich. When the body of a young boy, William, was found stabbed to death in the woods, the Jews of Norwich, England, were accused of ritual murder. In this instance, the Norwich Jews were alleged to have kidnapped William just before Easter:

> *And tortured him with all the tortures wherewith our Lord was tortured, and on Long Friday hanged him on a roof in hatred of our Lord.[149]*

Subsequent cases were recorded in Gloucester, England (1168); Blois, France (1171); Saragossa, Spain (1182); Bristol, England (1183); Fulda, Germany (1235); Lincoln, England (1255); and Munich, Germany (1286). Medieval poet Geoffrey Chaucer's "The Prioress's Tale" (in The Canterbury Tales) also invokes the blood libel motif, describing Jews as aroused by satanic urges to murder Christian children.

Blood libels were used in various parts of the world and have taken many forms, including the accusation that Jews use the blood of Christian children in their Passover rituals or that they kidnap and kill Christian children to use their blood in other religious ceremonies. These accusations are, of course, completely baseless and have no basis in facts. Still, they have been used by Christians to incite violence and persecution against Jews throughout history.

Shepherds' Crusade (1251)

The Shepherds' Crusade was a popular uprising in France in 1251. It was named after a shepherd who claimed to have had a vision from God instructing him to lead a crusade against the infidels and reclaim the Holy Land. A group of 60,000 followed him. The Shepherd's Crusade was a spontaneous and poorly organized movement that attracted a large following of peasants and lower-class people, who were drawn to the crusade by the promise of adventure, the chance to escape poverty and oppression, the promise to become heroes, and the hope of absolving their sins by participating in a holy cause. The crusade, while killing Jews and Muslims alike, was ultimately unsuccessful, and many of the participants were killed or captured by the Muslims in the Holy Land.

The Pastoureaux of 1320

Once again, a group of young Shepherds participated in a popular uprising in France in 1320. It was inspired after a teenage shepherd said he was visited by the Holy Spirit.[150] The Pastoureaux were predominantly from the lower classes, and they were motivated by a sense of religious fervor and a desire to bring about the end of the world. 40,000 French shepherds marched through France and parts of Europe, claiming to be on a holy mission and seeking to convert people to their cause. Many participants were killed or captured, and the movement quickly dissipated not before 140 Jewish communities in their path were destroyed. The following year, in Guienne, France, Jews were accused of prompting criminals to poison wells. 5,000 Jews were burned alive at the stake.

The Black Plague (1348-9)

The Black Plague, a devastating pandemic that swept through Europe in the mid-14th century, led to the deaths of roughly one-third of the continent's population. Amid this catastrophe, Jews were wrongly scapegoated and blamed for the disaster. False accusations claimed that Jews had poisoned wells, leading to widespread torture and murder of Jews from Spain to Poland.

At the time, the true cause of the plague and its mode of transmission was unknown, allowing rumors and myths about Jewish involvement to spread. Many Christians believed these baseless allegations, partly because the Jewish population seemed less affected by the plague than their Gentile counterparts. This discrepancy was primarily due to the Jewish people's strict adherence to biblical sanitary laws and Jewish purification rituals, which somewhat shielded them from the disease's devastating effects.

These unfounded accusations had dire consequences for Jewish communities across Europe. Over sixty Jewish communities were completely destroyed, with all their inhabitants killed. In some areas, Jews were subjected to torture and horrifically burned to death in large bonfires. The circulation of these false claims and the ensuing persecution exacerbated antisemitic sentiment throughout Europe, intensifying the marginalization and discrimination that Jews had long endured.[151]

The Spanish Inquisition (1483-1497)

Spain experienced the most significant evolution of Christian racial ideology during the fifteenth and sixteenth centuries.[152] Léon Poliakov has observed that Spanish theologians developed a doctrine positing that the erroneous beliefs of Jews had tarnished even their most distant descendants. The theologians argued that denying Christ for so long had biologically corrupted the Jews, even the conversos.[153] When Spanish Jews forcefully converted to Christianity and legal discrimination ceased, a considerable number of the approximately one million conversos (Jewish converts) thrived in Spanish society. Although the majority of conversos hailed from humble backgrounds, some achieved prominence in various fields, including the judiciary, municipal and national government bureaucracy, tax collection, military, universities, and the Church. Old Christians sought to eliminate competition from successful conversos by legally defining their origin-based impediments.[154] Yosef Yerushalmi, a professor of Jewish History at Columbia University, has noted that the traditional suspicion of Jews as outsiders was replaced by a more insidious fear of conversos as insiders.[155]

Spanish theologians concurred that the "despicable" ideas and religious motivations of Jews had so debased their descendants that all Jews were immune to baptism and salvation, being consumed by the "proverbially 'Jewish' traits of cunning, astuteness, and an insatiable desire for wealth and power, unencumbered by moral constraints."[156] By the sixteenth century, when nearly all remnants of Spanish crypto-Judaism had vanished, King Philip II, Popes Pius V, Sixtus V, and Clement VIII endorsed race laws predicated on the Jews' "mala sangre," or "bad blood."[157] At the same time, Old Christians were extolled for their "Limpieza de sangre," or "blood purity." Spanish race laws—"estatutos de limpieza de sangre"— applied to all conversos. A contemporary play lauded a "noble dog" that could sniff out Jews disguised in Christian attire. In 1604, Father Prudencio de Sandoval wrote that no one can deny that in the descendants of the Jews, there persists and endures the evil inclination of their ancient ingratitude and lack of understanding and that just one Jewish ancestor is enough to defile and corrupt a person.[158]

In 1623, a Portuguese scholar asserted that "a little Jewish blood is enough to destroy the world."[159] Francisco de Torrejoncillo was a Spanish Franciscan friar who lived in the 17th century. He is best known for his work "Centinela contra Judíos" ("Sentinel Against Jews"), a text written in 1674 that propagated anti-Jewish sentiments. After labeling Jews carnal, hedonistic, and cruel, he cautioned

Catholics: "There is no evil that the Jews do not desire, as they await their messiah. To be enemies of Christians, of Christ, and of his Divine Law, it is not necessary to be of a Jewish father and mother. One alone suffices."[160] Christian children must not "be suckled by Jewish vileness because that milk, being of infected persons, can only engender perverse inclinations."[161] Spanish racism was so pervasive that, with the exception of the Jesuits, all major Catholic orders in Spain during the sixteenth century adopted racist regulations to exclude individuals of Jewish descent from their brotherhood.[162]

In 1608, the Sixth General Congregation of the order decreed that no candidate could join the Society of Jesus unless their Gentile ancestry could be traced back five generations. Even the General of the Order could not waive this "impediment of origin," which persisted until 1946.[163] In 1935, the Jesuits condemned Hitler for adhering to the same "purity of blood" principle that the order itself had followed.[164]

Any extension of Spanish race laws to Catholic orders necessitated papal approval; when the majority of an order sought to exclude conversos, most popes ratified the rule.[165] Even the National-Socialist Nuremberg Decrees of 1935 were less exclusionary, defining a Jew as having one parent or two grandparents who were Jewish by religious identity. In the early sixteenth century, Pope Julius II, the warrior pope, reversed the racist momentum, describing such discrimination as "detestable and corrupt and contrary to the wishes of Christ and Paul."[166] In 1588 and 1600, Popes Sixtus V and Clement VIII approved a Portuguese law that prohibited men from Jewish families from being ordained as priests.[167]

The Spanish Inquisition was a period of religious and cultural persecution that took place in Spain and its colonies during the 15th and 16th centuries. Initiated by Pope Sixtus IV in 1478, who granted the Spanish monarchs, Ferdinand and Isabella, the authority to establish a special inquisition, the Catholic Church aimed to suppress heretical beliefs and practices, maintain the purity of the faith, and enforce religious and ideological conformity.

During this dark period, Jews, Muslims, and other minority groups were targeted and subjected to violence and persecution. Antisemitism played a significant role, as Jews were seen as a religious and cultural threat to the Catholic Church and its efforts to maintain control over Spain. Jews in Spain had a long history of persecution and discrimination, facing restrictions on their rights and freedoms, such as being forced to live in separate neighborhoods, known as ghettos, and being banned from certain occupations or professions.

The Spanish Inquisition specifically targeted Jewish conversos, who were suspected of secretly continuing to practice Jewish holidays and practices such as keeping kosher. Thousands of Jews were burned at the stake by the inquisitors' orders, accused of heresy, forced to convert to Catholicism, or subjected to torture and execution.

In 1492, King Ferdinand and Queen Isabella decided that all Jews should be expelled from Spain to further safeguard the Christian faith, resulting in the forced displacement of approximately 150,000 Jews from their homes.[168] They faced the difficult choice between conversion to Christianity or exile.

Many Jews who converted to Christianity continued to observe Jewish customs in secret and were referred to as "Marranos," a derogatory term derived from the Spanish word "Marrajo," meaning "pig." Those who chose exile sought refuge in neighboring countries such as Portugal, North Africa, and the Ottoman Empire. The expulsion of the Jews from Spain led to the loss of a rich cultural, intellectual, and economic resource, as well as causing immense human suffering.

The Spanish Inquisition and the subsequent expulsion of the Jews from Spain are a stark reminder of the dangers of religious intolerance, discrimination, and the abuse of power.

The anti-Jewish racial notions diffused from Spain throughout Europe. Erasmus, the Dutch man of letters and critic of Church excesses, contended that Christians must exercise caution when admitting Jews into the Church's fellowship, as a wholly converted Jew was an impossibility: the Jew would always remain pernicious. Erasmus wrote that the Jewish apostate Johannes Pfefferkorn, "appears quite typical of his race. His ancestors attacked Christ only, whereas he has [betrayed] Christendom, hypocritically claiming to have become a Christian. This half-Jew has done more harm to Christendom than all the Jews combined."[169]

Ulrich von Hutten, one of the authors of Letters of Obscure Men, similarly described Pfefferkorn:

> *Germany could not have produced such a monster. His parents are Jews, and he remains such, even if he has plunged his unworthy body into the baptism of Christ.*[170]

The apostate Jew and Pfefferkorn's friend, Victor von Karben, testified that many Christians ridiculed Pfefferkorn as a baptized Jew, stating, "Anything that is done for you is a waste. [Jews] will never become good Christians... Though you act like a Christian, you are still a Jew at heart."[171]

Martin Luther (1483-1546)

Martin Luther was a German theologian and religious reformer who initiated the Protestant Reformation in the 16th century. Regrettably, the reformation did not bring about a reformation in attitudes toward Jews. In fact, the animosity toward the Jewish people was reinforced and intensified by the reformers' writings, especially Martin Luther, the very man who initiated the Reformation.

At first, Luther showed some sympathy toward the Jews, believing that their rejection of the Gospel was a result of their awareness of the corruption within the Roman Catholic Church. However, when they rejected Luther's attempts at converting them, his attitude shifted dramatically:

> *They have failed to learn any lesson from the terrible distress that has been theirs for over fourteen hundred years in exile. If these blows do not help, it is reasonable to assume that our talking and explaining will help even less. Much less do I propose to convert the Jews, for that is impossible.*[172]

Luther wrote of the Jews as a "race" that could not genuinely convert to Christianity. By portraying the Jews as the devil's people, Luther placed them beyond the possibility of conversion. He argued that attempting to convert Jews was akin to "trying to cast out the devil."[173] In his sermon given on September 25, 1539, Luther demonstrated through several examples that individual Jews could not convert permanently.[174]

In multiple passages of Luther's "On the Jews and Their Lies," Luther seemed to reject the notion that Jews would or could convert:

> *Dear Christian, be advised and so not doubt that next to the devil, you have no more bitter, venomous, and vehement foe than a real Jew who earnestly seeks to be a Jew... Their lineage and circumcision infect them all. A Jewish heart is as hard as stone and iron and cannot be moved by any means. Even if the Jews were punished in the most gruesome manner so that the streets ran with blood, so that their dead would be counted not in the hundred thousands but in the millions, [it would not be] possible to convert these children of the devil! It is impossible to convert the devil and his own, nor are we commanded to attempt this.[175]*

This document also contained vehement anti-Semitic sentiments. In it, he referred to the Jews in a derogatory manner, expressing his disappointment and anger at their refusal to accept the Gospel:[176]

> *For such ruthless wrath of God is sufficient evidence that they [the Jewish people] assuredly have erred and gone astray. Even a child can comprehend this. For one dare not regard God as so cruel that he would punish his own people so long, so terrible, so unmercifully. Therefore, this work of wrath is proof that the Jews, surely rejected by God, are no longer his people, and neither is he any longer their God.[177]*

Martin Luther also wrote:

> *What then shall we Christians do with this damned, rejected race of Jews? Since they live among us and we know about their lying and blasphemy and cursing, we can not tolerate them if we do not wish to share in their lies, curses, and blasphemy. In this way we cannot quench*

the inextinguishable fire of divine rage nor convert the Jews. We must prayerfully and reverentially practice a merciful severity. Perhaps we may save a few from the fire and flames [of hell]. We must not seek vengeance. They are surely being punished a thousand times more than we might wish them. Let me give you my honest advice.

First, their synagogues should be set on fire, and whatever does not burn up should be covered or spread over with dirt so that no one may ever be able to see a cinder or stone of it. And this ought to be done for the honor of God and of Christianity in order that God may see that we are Christians, and that we have not wittingly tolerated or approved of such public lying, cursing, and blaspheming of His Son and His Christians.

Secondly, their homes should likewise be broken down and destroyed. For they perpetrate the same things there that they do in their synagogues. For this reason they ought to be put under one roof or in a stable, like gypsies, in order that they may realize that they are not masters in our land, as they boast, but miserable captives, as they complain of incessantly before God with bitter wailing.

Thirdly, they should be deprived of their prayer-books and Talmuds in which such idolatry, lies, cursing, and blasphemy are taught.

Fourthly, their rabbis must be forbidden under threat of death to teach any more...

Fifthly, passport and traveling privileges should be absolutely forbidden to the Jews. For they have no business in the rural districts since they are not nobles, nor officials, nor merchants, nor the like. Let them stay at home...If you princes and nobles do not close the road legally to such exploiters, then some troop ought to ride against them, for they will learn from this pamphlet what the Jews are and how to handle them and that they ought not to be protected. You ought not, you cannot protect them, unless in the eyes of God you want to share all their abomination...

To sum up, dear princes and nobles who have Jews in your domains, if this advice of mine does not suit you, then find a better one so that you and we may all be free of this insufferable devilish burden - the Jews...

Let the government deal with them in this respect, as I have suggested. But whether the government acts or not, let everyone at least be guided by his own conscience and form for himself a definition or image of a Jew. When you lay eyes on or think of a Jew you must say to yourself: Alas, that mouth which I there behold has cursed and execrated and maligned every Saturday my dear Lord Jesus Christ, who has redeemed me with his precious blood; in addition, it prayed and pleaded before God that I, my wife and children, and all Christians might be stabbed to death and perish miserably. And he himself would gladly do this if he were able, in order to appropriate our goods...

Such a desperate, thoroughly evil, poisonous, and devilish lot are these Jews, who for these fourteen hundred years have been and still are our plague, our pestilence, and our misfortune.

I have read and heard many stories about the Jews which agree with this judgment of Christ,

> *namely, how they have poisoned wells, made assassinations, kidnapped children, as related before. I have heard that one Jew sent another Jew, and this by means of a Christian, a pot of blood, together with a barrel of wine, in which when drunk empty, a dead Jew was found. There are many other similar stories. For their kidnapping of children they have often been burned at the stake or banished (as we already heard). I am well aware that they deny all of this. However, it all coincides with the judgment of Christ which declares that they are venomous, bitter, vindictive, tricky serpents, assassins, and children of the devil, who sting and work harm stealthily wherever they cannot do it openly. For this reason, I would like to see them where there are no Christians. The Turks and other heathen do not tolerate what we Christians endure from these venomous serpents and young devils...next to the devil, a Christian has no more bitter and galling foe than a Jew. There is no other to whom we accord as many benefactions and from whom we suffer as much as we do from these base children of the devil, this brood of vipers.[178]*

This, to remind us, is the father of the reformation. Martin Luther's work not only perpetuated existing prejudices but also added much fuel to the fire of anti-Semitism, which would continue to have a devastating impact on Jewish communities for centuries to come and set the stage for the Holocaust.

Undeniably, the Nazis used Luther's writings as they rose to power and initiated the Holocaust. In his famous book, Mein Kampf, published in 1925, Adolf Hitler praised Martin Luther as "a great warrior, a true statesman, and a great reformer."

Hitler, too, claimed to be a Christian. In 1924, at a Christian gathering in Berlin, Hitler spoke to thousands and received a standing ovation when he made the following declaration:

> *I believe that today I am acting in accordance with the will of Almighty God as I announce the most important work that Christians could undertake — and that is to be against the Jews and get rid of them once and for all.*[179]

Hitler then proceeded to discuss the great impact Luther had on his life:

> *Martin Luther has been the greatest encouragement of my life. Luther was a great man. He was a giant. With one blow he heralded the coming of the new dawn and the new age. He saw clearly that the Jews need to be destroyed, and we're only beginning to see that we need to carry this work on.*[180]

It may be shocking, but Hitler's views, as extreme as they were, didn't differ significantly from those held by many Christians throughout history. The key distinction is that Hitler had the means to implement these deeply ingrained ideas.

In fact, at the Nuremberg trials, the Nazi leader Julius Streicher, who was third-highest rank in the Nazi leadership, defended himself by asserting:

> *I have never said anything that Martin Luther did not say.*[181]

The painful truth that many Christians are reluctant to confront, and which some are unaware of, is that the Holocaust was the culmination of nearly 1,900 years of persistent Christian anti-Semitism. Acknowledging this dark chapter in history is hard yet crucial for ensuring such atrocities won't occur again.

Sure, Martin Luther introduced a significant Jewish value into Christianity, which is the truth that we do not need to earn the love of our Heavenly Father; instead, we simply need to acknowledge it. However, it is ironic that he failed to grasp the full implications of that love when he turned against the Jews with hatred and contempt.

John Calvin (1509-64)
John Calvin was a French theologian, pastor, and influential figure in the development of the Protestant Reformation, particularly known for his controversial doctrine of predestination and his role in shaping the Reformed branch of Christianity known as "Calvinism." Much like Martin Luther, Calvin had great contemptuousness toward the Jewish people. For instance:

> *[The Jews'] rotten and unbending stiffneckedness deserves that they be oppressed unendingly and without measure or end and that they die in their misery without the pity of anyone!*[182]

The Portuguese Inquisition (1536-1821)
The Portuguese Inquisition was a religious tribunal primarily aimed at maintaining Catholic orthodoxy in the empire and enforcing religious conformity among its citizens. The tribunal was officially established in Portugal in 1536, following the models of the Spanish Inquisition. However, the seeds of the Inquisition in Portugal were sown earlier in 1497 when King Manuel I decreed that all Jews should convert to Christianity or leave the country.

Jews who chose to convert were known as "New Christians" or "Conversos." However, many of these converts secretly continued to practice Judaism. These individuals were referred to as "crypto-Jews" or "Marranos." The Portuguese Inquisition was particularly harsh towards the Jews, accusing them of heresy for their secret continuation of Jewish practices and beliefs.

Jews were targeted by the Inquisition due to the prevailing anti-Semitic sentiments and the religious intolerance of the time. They were often subjected to harsh punishments such as torture, confiscation of property, and execution.

The effects of the Portuguese Inquisition on the Jewish community were devastating. Many Jews were forced to flee the country to escape persecution, leading to a significant Jewish diaspora in other parts of the world, including Asia, North Africa, the Ottoman Empire, Western Europe, and the Americas.

One such example is Goa, India, once a British and Portuguese colony. The locals in Goa continued targeting "heretics," which extended to the crypto-Jews who fled Portugal. Similar to the experience in Portugal, this led to persecution and the ultimate dissolution of established Jewish communities:

> *Over time, the Inquisition tribunal in Goa morphed into a mechanism for land grabbing. Wealthy Jewish merchants and affluent local Hindus alike faced persecution. The synagogues of Old Goa did not survive the 252-year-long Inquisition, leading to the cessation of the Jewish settlement. The Goa tribunal was set up for the purpose of punishing the "heretics." Those who had left Portugal for a new life in Goa, men who were not considered "proper Catholics" but were accused of being Judaizers.*[183]

Cossack Massacre (1648-49)

"Cossack massacre" refers to several violent conflicts involving Cossacks, a group of semi-nomadic warriors and peasants living in Europe and Asia's borderlands in the early modern period. Cossacks were known for their martial skills and willingness to engage in violent confrontations, and they were involved in several conflicts throughout history. Massacres were carried out by Bogdan Chmielnicki, leader of the Cossacks. During the peasant revolt against Polish rule in Ukraine, over 100,000 Jews were killed, and 300 communities were destroyed.

Modern Period Antisemitism

The Pogroms (19th-20th centuries)
Antisemitism has played a significant role in the history of pogroms, as Jews have often been the victims of violent attacks and persecution motivated by negative stereotypes and prejudices about their religion and culture. Pogroms against Jews have taken place in various parts of the world and have often been fueled by various factors, including political, social, and economic tensions.

One of the most well-known examples of pogroms against Jews is the Russian pogroms of the late 19th and early 20th centuries, characterized by widespread violence and persecution of Jews by Christians in the Russian Empire. These pogroms were often instigated by the authorities or by mobs of people. Between 1881-84, numerous pogroms occurred in more than 100 Jewish villages in southern Russia, with looting, rape, and murder. These violent acts prompted a Jewish exit from Russia; many fled to America.

Pogroms against Jews have also occurred in other parts of the world, including Europe, the Middle East, and North Africa. These attacks have often been characterized by extreme violence. Overall, pogroms have been a tragic and devastating feature of human history and have been used to persecute and discriminate against a range of minority groups, mainly Jews.

Easter Riot in Moldova (1903)
Jews were falsely accused of causing the death of a murdered Christian child and a young Christian woman who had committed suicide at a hospital with Jewish staff. Subsequently, during Easter, violence broke out, killing 49 Jews and leaving about 500 injured. It was later discovered that the child had been killed by relatives, and the suicide was unrelated to the Jewish community.

Discrimination in the United States of America (1920s)
In North America, anti-Jewish prejudice became pervasive. Numerous universities implemented quotas for Jewish students. For instance, when Harvard admitted students based on merit alone, the Jewish student population was around 15%. However, by 1941, after implementing quotas, Most Universities' Jewish student population fell to less than 2%. Jews were also commonly excluded from

Protestant country clubs, restricted neighborhoods, and other Protestant-dominated areas.

Kristallnacht (1938)

Kristallnacht, also known as "the Night of Broken Glass," was a violent riot that took place on November 9 and 10, 1938. It was a coordinated attack on the Jewish population of Germany and Austria, in which synagogues, Jewish-owned businesses, and homes were vandalized, looted, and burned.

Kristallnacht was a turning point in the history of the Holocaust, as it marked the beginning of a more systematic and widespread campaign of violence and persecution against the Jews. The pogrom was instigated by the Nazi Party and carried out by SA stormtroopers (paramilitary units) and other Nazi supporters, and it resulted in the deaths of at least 91 Jews, the arrest of more than 30,000 Jewish men, and the destruction of thousands of Jewish homes and businesses.

Kristallnacht was a horrific event motivated by anti-Semitic hatred and the desire to terrorize and demoralize the Jewish population.

French Jewish Deportation (1940)

The French Jewish Deportation refers to the deportation of Jews from France to concentration camps during the Holocaust, whereby the Vichy government of France collaborated with Nazi Germany. This process began in 1940 and lasted until the end of World War II in 1945. During this period, the Nazi regime and its collaborators in France implemented policies of persecution and extermination against the Jewish population, which included measures such as the forced wearing of the yellow star, the confiscation of Jewish-owned property, and the mass arrest and deportation of Jews to concentration camps.

The French Jewish Deportation is considered one of the darkest chapters in the history of France. An estimated 76,000 Jews were deported from France to concentration camps during the Holocaust; of these, only 2,500 survived.

The Holocaust (1939-1945)

Without the poisoning of Christian minds through the centuries, the Holocaust is unthinkable.
(Robert Runcie, Archbishop of Canterbury)[184]

During the 19th and early 20th centuries, Christian antisemitism took on new forms due to the rise of racial theories that characterized Jews as inferior. In Europe, these attitudes were fueled by the increase of antisemitic political movements, such as the Nazi Party in Germany, which perpetrated the Holocaust.

It is essential to recognize that Christian antisemitism is not inherent to Christianity itself but rather is a perversion of the teachings of Jesus and the principles of love, justice, and compassion central to the genuine Christian faith. Christians must work to combat racism and antisemitism within their own communities and stand in solidarity with Jews in the face of prejudice and discrimination. Only by acknowledging and addressing the dark history of Christian antisemitism can we hope to build a more just and harmonious world for all people. As the famous phrase goes: "Those that fail to learn from history are doomed to repeat it."[185]

A comprehensive understanding of history is indispensable for individuals to truly comprehend their identities and make informed decisions for their present and future. Every person has been influenced by the values and institutions they have inherited from the past. Among these, religion has played a pivotal role in shaping fundamentally spiritual people. Even those not actively engaged in the profound theological questions of life and death, good and evil, or right and wrong are still emotionally entwined with these concepts and frequently base their critical choices on beliefs, values, and attitudes passed down to them, particularly in the pre-modern Western world, by the Churches and their theologians.

Leading to the Holocaust

The Holocaust stands out as one of the most incomprehensible events in history. Scholars especially acknowledge the limitations of historical explanation. Nevertheless, just as historians attempt to explain phenomena such as the decline and fall of Rome or the origins of the First World War, they strive to decipher the enigma and fathom the depths of the Holocaust, seeking to understand why it occurred. As a theologian, I would argue for a supernatural evil dimension operating behind the scenes to promote anti-Semitism to destroy the Jews. Remember, when the Jews finally accept Christ (Matthew 23:39; Romans 11:25-26), it is "game over" for the devil. Therefore, what better solution than the "final solution," eliminating his Jewish threat altogether? Interestingly, from all people groups, the devil was crafty enough to use Christianity to try and destroy the Jews.

There is a lesson here for us. Satan used scripture to try to tempt and deceive Jesus. If the devil thought it would be a good idea to use the Bible to manipulate Christ, we can rest assured he is also using it to manipulate and deceive us. Therefore, the best way for Satan to attack the gospel is by manipulating the Bible. Satan has convinced many Christians that they are being "biblical" when they cherry-pick verses, usually taken out of context, that align with their agenda and preconceived ideas. This trickery leads them to believe that they are following Christ when in fact, they are harming the gospel and causing people—not only Jews—to reject it. If this is true, and considering how Satan operates, it probably is, then many of the people who need redemption are already inside the church. However, they require redeeming from misguided beliefs perpetuated on them by other Christians around them who believe they are being "biblical." While antisemitism is a grand example, we should ask ourselves what other Christian doctrines have been infected as well.

While we will soon explore the impact of Christianity on the Holocaust, it can be said upfront that two millennia of Christian ideas and prejudices, and their influence on Christians' actions, form the primary foundation of antisemitism and its culmination in the Holocaust.

In the initial centuries of the Christian era, pre-existing pagan animosity towards Jews (with approximately a quarter of pagan writers harboring hostility towards Jews due to their inability to comprehend Jewish monotheism and practices such as the Sabbath, circumcision, and kosher foods) was supplanted by the belief that all Jews were eternally culpable for the murder of God. Consequently, the Jewish people were deemed repugnant, and any injustice inflicted upon them—murder included, according to some church fathers—was justifiable. The "deicidal" Jews were established as the quintessential malefactors in Christian societies, and this anti-Jewish sentiment became a constant element in the core identity of Western Christian civilization. Christian authors like Martin Luther reinterpreted Jewish virtues as vices and their values as sins, proclaiming that "evil [was] good and good evil...everything was completely turned upside-down."[186] This theology posited that the Christian Church, the "new Israel"—divinely ordained and endorsed—had superseded the cursed and forsaken old Israel in moral, historical, and metaphysical terms. This ideology, often referred to as triumphalism, viewed the entire Jewish race as inherently wicked who had, long before the birth of Jesus, slaughtered their prophets and then betrayed and assassinated their true Messiah for money. These notions dominated Christianity's stance on Judaism and Jews for two millennia. As Prof. Jacob Neusner observed:

At no time before our own century did Christianity contemplate Judaism as an equal.[187]

Once the theological schism between Christianity and Judaism occurred in the first century of the Common Era and was politically solidified in the fourth century, the Church endeavored to establish its distinct identity from Judaism as autonomously as possible. To achieve this, the Church cast the Jews as outsiders, aberrations, and social outcasts. The predominant teachings of many Christian church leaders about Jews revolved around the story of Cain and Abel. However, the moral lesson was not about being our brothers' keepers; instead, it centered on the notion, originating from Augustine, that all Jews were Cains—with Jewishness and Judaism as their stigmata—and that Jews' destiny was to wander as suffering examples of what it meant to reject and murder God.

For two millennia, Christian theology, institutionalized in the Churches, has been the most profound source of hostility towards Jews, Judaism, and Jewishness. The church has, by far, been the most significant instrument of Jewish suffering than all other causes.

However, another type of Christian ideology coexisted with Theologia Gloriae. This was a liberal ideology that called for ethical Christian treatment of all humans and is known as the Theology of the Cross ("Theologia Crucis"), based on Jesus' statement in the Gospel of Matthew (16:24-25). This belief mandated that Christians should follow the moral teachings of Jesus concerning all humans, even at the risk of their own lives.

Emphasizing Jesus' humanity, his fears, anxieties, and his courage and faith, the theology of the cross highlights the shared suffering among all human beings, both Gentile and Jew. An analysis of Christians who aided Jews during the Holocaust, such as Corrie Ten Boom, reveals that motivation. Unfortunately, these individuals were few and far between.

Conversely, during the Holocaust, most Christian Churches and their followers did not adhere to "Theologia Crucis," as they either remained silent or collaborated while Jews were taken away to the labor camps and crematories, oftentimes by other Christians. This Christian silence justified the murder of Christianity's brothers by the authority of Christianity (the churches, culture, theology, art, education, etc.). In this manner, many Christians directly or indirectly became what they professed to despise: murderous Cains.

[The Holocaust] would not have been possible without the almost two thousand years' pre-history of 'Christian' anti-Judaism[188]
(Swiss priest Hans Küng)

Distinguished figures such as Karl Barth and Hannah Arendt regarded the association between the Christian Churches and the Holocaust as inconceivable.[189] The moral principles of the Churches, starkly contrasting with the genocidal morality of Nazi Germany, were thought to negate any connection between Christian doctrines and the Final Solution. However, those who argue that Christianity played an indispensable role in the genesis of the Holocaust do not refer to Jesus' moral teachings but to later Christian ideology, starting with the Church Fathers, that harbors contempt and animosity toward all things Jewish.

Just as much as the rejection of Christ serves as a pillar in Jewish theology, so does the hatred of the Jew served as a pillar in Christian theology for most of the past two thousand years.

This sheds light on why individuals—nearly all born into Christianity, baptized and married in a church, and ultimately buried in consecrated ground, originating from a Christian environment, and imbibing a form of Christian culture that denounced Jews—endeavored to exterminate all Jews in Europe during the Holocaust.

Additionally, it explains why many Christians either actively participated in this murderous undertaking or tacitly allowed it to transpire.

In his introduction to Lessons and Legacies,[190] Peter Hayes poses two central questions: "How could [Christian] people permit such things?" and "Why did so few courageous individuals attempt to intercede?" The answer lies in the fact that the majority of European Christians—not only in Germany—collaborated actively or passively, to varying degrees, with Hitler's objectives, not solely due to the pressures of fear and anxiety but also because a millennial anti-Jewish Christian ideology had predisposed them to antisemitism.

Almost every Nazi administrative directive—from yellow stars to ghettos, from defamations to deportations, from round-ups to massacres—had a precedent in the Christian West.[191] Millions of Jews had already been murdered by Christians in Europe before Adolf Hitler's birth. Jews were vilified as devils since the Church Fathers' time and systematically slaughtered from the Middle Ages onward.[192] Amidst the Dreyfus Affair, 20,000 French Catholics—often writing on behalf of their children and pets—expressed their intent to flay, butcher, and boil the alleged Jewish vampires alive or to bake them in Baccarat ovens. Abbé Cros donated three francs for a bedside rug made from "Yids' [Jewish] skins to trample on morning and evenings."[193] They referred to Jews as bugs.

A generation later, Nazi Germany and their collaborators treated Jews like insects, exterminating millions using an insecticide called Zyklon. The Nazis integrated a comprehensive organization, fanatical commitment, and technology to actualize the murderous impulses intrinsic to Christian antisemitism to a horrifying extent.

Richard Steigmann-Gall emphasizes that Nazism was not fundamentally an anti-Christian pagan movement[194] and that

Christianity played a vital role in most Nazis' lives and their Nazism.

Ironically, during the Holocaust, my grandmother was captured and taken to a concentration camp, where she was tortured and told it was because she, as a Jew, had killed Christ. Yet when Christmas time arrived, she and her Jewish friends in the concentration camp would hear the Nazi soldiers outside singing Christmas carols on their way to church, celebrating the birth of Christ, who was, in fact, Jewish.

Christians believed the Jewishness of Germany's troubles necessitated a "final solution" to these Jewish-induced problems. The so-called Nazi pagans—whom many Christian Nazis opposed—were anti-ecclesiastical but not anti-Christian. Nazi antisemitism aligned seamlessly with Christian antisemitism, as leading Nazis professed Protestant Christianity. In their social policies, Nazis were guided by a Christian ethic. Ultimately, Nazism may have been hostile at times to the churches but never "uniformly anti-Christian."[195] Numerous Nazis, both Catholic and Protestant, adhered to "Positive Christianity," in which they adopted a divine Jesus Christ as the foremost antisemite. They asserted themselves to be genuine Christians beyond the artificial division of Catholic and Protestant denominations, claiming that Christianity was a central aspect of their movement and shaped its direction and worldview.[196]

Alfred Rosenberg, the Nazi "pagan," referred to Jesus as the "lynchpin of [German] history... God of the Europeans."[197] Ideology alone did not cause the Nazi Holocaust. A confluence of political, economic, military, and psychosocial factors also contributed.[198] However, the anti-Jewish aspects of Christian thought, theology, the anti-Jewish Christian ideology and attitudes, and the anti-Jewish precedents provided by the churches' historical relationship with Jews significantly influenced and may have determined the conception, establishment, and execution of the Holocaust.

The churches and their theologians had formulated persuasive religious, social, and moral ideas that offered a conceptual framework for perceiving Jews as subhuman or as inhuman, diabolical, and satanic. These churches and theologians had labeled Jews as traitors, murderers, plague, pollution, filth, and insects long before the Nazis identified Jews similarly.

From the earliest centuries of the Common Era, many Christians discovered an inherent theological repugnance, as well as "a horrible and fascinating physical otherness" in Jews.[199] In 1941, K.E. Robinson, an official of the British Colonial Office, deemed Jews "entirely alien in every sense of the word."[200]

Nazi Germany and Christianity

Humans tend to forget, and unfortunately, we live in a generation that is unaware of the truths regarding the Holocaust, as "nearly two-thirds of US young adults unaware six million Jews killed in the Holocaust,"[201] and many of which even "said they believed the Holocaust was a myth."[202]

No one can deny that antisemitism significantly fueled and enabled the Holocaust, the systematic extermination of approximately six million Jews by the Nazi regime and its collaborators during World War II.

Antisemitism has a long and complex history and has taken many forms over the centuries, including violence, persecution, and discrimination. In the 19th and early 20th centuries, antisemitism was a widespread and influential ideology, and it was embraced by many people, including politicians, intellectuals, and ordinary citizens.

The Nazi regime in Germany, which came to power in 1933, used antisemitism as a central component of its ideology and policies. The Nazis used propaganda and other forms of manipulation to spread and reinforce negative stereotypes about Jews that were already there, portraying them as a threat to the "Aryan" race and the German nation.

Nazi Germany and its supporters sought to create a connection between the Aryan race and Christianity to justify their beliefs in racial superiority and further their political aims. They promoted a version of Christianity called "Positive Christianity," which was meant to blend traditional Christian beliefs with Nazi racial ideology. This included the idea that Jesus was an Aryan and that the Aryan race was divinely chosen.

Adolf Hitler used the term "Positive Christianity" in point 24 of the 1920 Nazi Party Platform, stating: "The Party as such represents the viewpoint of Positive Christianity without binding itself to any particular denomination."[203]

In another speech, Hitler declared himself "a German Christian."[204]

Later, the "Christian Identity Movement," a far-right, white supremacist movement, emerged in the United States in the 20th century. Adherents of Christian Identity believe that white Europeans, particularly those of Anglo-Saxon, Celtic, and Nordic descent, are the true Israelites mentioned in the Bible and are God's chosen people. They argue that non-white races are inferior and that Jews are the offspring of Satan. In their interpretation, the Aryan race has a divine mandate to rule over other races. While these examples represent fringe belief systems, and their views are not representative of mainstream Christianity, this was what Jews in Europe kept hearing about Jesus and Christianity.

The Holocaust was a systematic and organized effort to eliminate Jews from Europe and other parts of the world. The Nazi regime and its collaborators implemented a range of measures to target and persecute Jews, including legislation that restricted their rights and freedoms, forced labor, ghettos, concentration camps, and, ultimately, the use of extermination camps.

Antisemitism played a significant role in enabling and justifying the Holocaust, as it provided a framework for the Nazi regime to dehumanize and demonize Jews and justify their extermination.

In 1924 at a Christian gathering in Berlin, Hitler spoke to thousands and received a standing ovation when he made the following proclamation:

> *I believe that today I am acting in accordance with the will of Almighty God as I announce the most important work that Christians could undertake — and that is to be against the Jews and get rid of them once and for all.*[205]

In 1933 Martin Luther's wish finally came true. When Adolf Hitler met with Bishop Berning, Hitler told him:

> *I recognize the representatives of this [Jewish] race as pestilent for the state and for the church and perhaps I am thereby doing Christianity a great service for pushing them out of schools and public functions.*[206]

Under the Nazi regime in Germany, some Jews found that wearing a necklace with the cross of Jesus provided protection, as it helped conceal their Jewish identity from those who sought to harm them. It is a striking irony that the cross, a symbol intrinsically linked to Christianity, could serve as a shield to protect Jews from persecution and potential death by those who professed to be Christians. The cross symbolizes torture, persecution, and death for the Jewish people, not of Christ, but their own.

We, Jews, have learned to fear Christians just as much as mice fear cats. Christianity turned Jesus into Judaism's kryptonite, unknowingly serving Satan's agenda of keeping Jews from believing in Jesus.

Alongside criticism, it is essential to mention that in 1998 the Catholic Church addressed its anti-Semitic past. Pope John Paul II issued a document in which he, on behalf of the Catholic Church, asked for the forgiveness of the Jewish people, admitting that "the crime which has become known as the Holocaust remains an indelible stain..."[207] And in year 2,000, "In an unprecedented plea, Pope John Paul II today asked divine forgiveness for the sins committed by the Roman Catholic Church over the last 2,000 years against Jews.[208]

Though this cannot bring back the family members other Jewish families and I lost, it demonstrates a willingness to correct past wrongs and repent from these atrocities, which is worthy of appreciation.

Pope Benedict XVI, the successor to John Paul II, took this sentiment further by reminding Catholics that, like Jesus and those who followed him, the entire early Christian community mainly comprised Jews. He also rejected the idea of collective Jewish guilt for Jesus Christ's death.[209]

We can only hope that other denominations will also follow in this direction.

For two thousand years, Christian persecution of Jews has created the impression that Jesus sought their destruction. However, Jesus did not come to take lives but to offer His life through his own sacrifice. This action exemplifies God's love—a love willing to surrender everything for the benefit of Jews and Gentiles alike. Such love should be demonstrated towards all, Jews included, by those who proclaim to follow Christ.

Things have taken a serious turn. To bring some positivity back into the atmosphere, I have another Jewish joke for you. You can access it by scanning the barcode below with your phone's camera or by typing the URL directly into your web browser:

www.eitan.bar/joke2

Modern-day Antisemitism

*We have understood, with horror,
that antisemitism is still alive.
And on this issue, our response must be
unforgiving.
(Emanuel Macron, President of France)*

After enduring two millennia of relentless persecution and antisemitism, it became imperative for the Jewish people to establish their own homeland. This would not only offer them a much-needed haven of security but also the freedom for self-determination. Moreover, it would serve as a sanctuary where they could preserve and celebrate their unique culture without the constant specter of fear.

The ancient Land of Israel was chosen as the location for this homeland because it holds deep historical, cultural, and religious significance for the Jewish people. The land of Israel is the ancestral home of the Jewish people, with a continuous Jewish presence dating back thousands of years. The region is central to Jewish religious beliefs and is the birthplace of Judaism.

Indeed, the modern State of Israel was established in 1948, following a United Nations resolution that aimed to create separate Jewish and Arab states in the region, allowing for the Jewish people to return to their historical homeland and establish a nation-state where they could live free from persecution.

After Israel was established in 1948, the country faced immediate challenges and conflicts. Neighboring Muslim states, which opposed the creation of a Jewish state in the region, launched an immediate military attack against Israel, leading to the first Arab-Israeli war, also known as the War of Independence.

Israel managed to defend its territory and even expand its borders during the conflict.

Since then, Israel has faced multiple wars, attacks, and periods of tension with its neighbors, such as the Suez Crisis (1956), the Six-Day War (1967), the Yom Kippur War (1973), and ongoing conflicts with

Palestinian groups. Despite these challenges, Israel has built a strong, thriving nation with a robust economy, advanced technology sector, and vibrant cultural scene. However, the region's path to peace and stability has been complex. It remains an ongoing pursuit, as thousands of Israeli (and Palestinian) civilians have been killed in conflicts, wars, and terrorist attacks since the establishment of the state in 1948.

Worldwide, modern-day antisemitism takes many forms, ranging from overt acts of violence and hate speech to more subtle forms of discrimination. One form of modern-day antisemitism is the use of hate speech and violence against Jews. This can include physical attacks on individuals or vandalism of Jewish property, such as synagogues and cemeteries. In recent years, there has been a disturbing rise in antisemitic violence and hate crimes, particularly in Europe and the United States.

Hatred towards the Jewish people persists in various forms. In 2019, antisemitic incidents rose by 74%,[210] and by 2020, they had increased by an additional 27%.[211] Europe and the U.S. have witnessed an alarming surge in violent acts against the Jewish community. This includes a 36 percent increase in 2022 in the US. Campus and school incidents up nearly 50 percent; 91 bomb threats targeting Jewish institutions.[212]

In some extreme cases, replacement theology directly contributed to evil acts of terror against Jews.[213,214] This makes it particularly challenging for Jewish individuals to distinguish between Christians who believe in replacement theology and Christians who don't.

Another form of modern-day antisemitism is using stereotypes and negative portrayals of Jews in media and popular culture. These can range from classic antisemitic tropes, such as the portrayal of Jews as greedy and manipulative who systematically try to take over the world, to more subtle forms of discrimination, such as the exclusion of Jews from certain roles, or the portrayal of Jewish characters in a negative light.

In addition to these more overt forms of antisemitism, there are also more subtle forms of discrimination against Jews. This can include the exclusion of Jews from certain social or professional circles or the use of language or policies that are disproportionately harmful to Jews.

One example is the "boycott, divestment, and sanctions" (BDS) movement, which aims to political and financial pressure Israel. While the BDS movement claims to be a nonviolent and human rights-based movement, some of its supporters have been accused of using antisemitic language and promoting antisemitic conspiracy theories. These conspiracy theories have no basis and are used to spread misinformation and sow division.

The devastating impact of the Holocaust has seemingly diminished the most extreme forms of anti-Semitism among Christian leaders. However, anti-Semitism persists in a modern, refined guise known as anti-Zionism. While traditional anti-Semitism aimed to expel Jews from the lands they inhabited, anti-Zionism now rejects their right to dwell in their own homeland. A prime example of this contemporary anti-Semitism is a document published by Dr. James Kennedy's Knox Theological Seminary in 2002, which has been endorsed by numerous theologians and pastors, including famous Calvinist theologian R.C. Sproul. This open letter to Evangelicals addresses the topic of Israel, denouncing the belief that biblical promises about the land are being fulfilled today for a single ethnic group.[215] The document contends that these promises "do not apply to any particular ethnic group but to the church of Jesus Christ, the true Israel."

Moreover, it denies the Jewish claim to any land: "The land promises specific to Israel in the Old Testament were fulfilled under Joshua."[216] And also, "The entitlement of any one ethnic or religious group to territory in the Middle East called the 'Holy Land' cannot be supported by Scripture." The document also asserts, "The present secular state of Israel… is not an authentic or prophetic realization."[217]

Since then, other reformed pastors have expressed the same sentiments. For example, John Piper wrote that because the Jews "broke covenant with their God," and therefore, "the secular state of Israel today may not claim a present divine right to the Land."[218]

BDS Movement

> *We have, in Israel, a thriving democracy, a beacon of tolerance, an engine of enterprise and an example to the rest of the world for overcoming adversity and defying disadvantages. It is only when you walk through Jerusalem or Tel Aviv that you see a country where people of all religions and sexualities are free and equal in the eyes of the law.*
>
> *The boycotts, divestment and sanctions movement is wrong, it is unacceptable, and this party and this government will have no truck with those who subscribe to it. Our focus is the opposite – on taking our trading and investing relationship with Israel to the next level.*
>
> *Antisemitism is racism. It has absolutely no place in our society and we must fight its bitter scourge wherever it rears its head. I've been proud to lead a government that is tackling such discrimination in all its forms – from making sure courts have the powers they need to deal with those who peddle hatred, to asking the Law Commission to undertake a full review of hate crime legislation. But there is yet more to do.*
> *(Theresa May, Former Prime Minister of the United Kingdom)*

I recognize that not everyone may agree with me. Still, I argue that the BDS movement is a modern antisemitic movement (propelled by an underlying Islamic agenda) which, unfortunately, is supported by many Christians who do not always understand BDS' true motives. The challenge in recognizing the BDS movement for what it truly arises from the movement's skillful manipulation of human rights language and the distortion of noble concepts like "justice" and "peace."

Far from seeking a peaceful resolution to the Israeli-Palestinian conflict, the BDS movement ultimately aims to dismantle Israel as we know it. BDS co-founder and leader Omar Barghouti occasionally reveals this intent: "We oppose a Jewish state in any part of Palestine."[219] Although BDS claims to advocate only non-violent measures, its proposals would dissolve the world's only Jewish state. Moreover, anyone familiar with the Middle East understands that realizing BDS's goals would spell disaster for the Jewish population. In a majority Palestinian state—likely led by Islamist groups like Hamas—Jews would face violence and oppression, as is common for minorities in the region. Those who argue that Jews could live securely in a majority Palestinian state are merely concealing their cynical intentions behind the guise of justice.

According to official British Mandatory estimates, both Christians and Jews used to live in Palestine. In fact, the Christian population in 1922 constituted about 10-15% of the Arab population. Today, Muslims are 99.5% in the Gaza Strip, while Palestinian Christians comprise approximately 0.5% only. No Jews live in Gaza anymore. Most Christians and all Jews either fled or were killed. It is not hard to imagine what would happen to the Jewish people if Muslim groups took over Israel.

Debating whether BDS or anti-Zionism is antisemitic is inherently flawed. How can calling for dismantling the world's only Jewish state not be antisemitic? Furthermore, even if one could distinguish between denying individual Jewish rights (antisemitic) and rejecting their collective rights (supposedly acceptable), we are still discussing the dismemberment of a UN Member State. Regardless of whether that state is Jewish or, say, Ukrainian - advocating for its end cannot be considered a legitimate political position.

Despite this, many Christian individuals, as well as Christian churches, such as the Presbyterian denomination,[220] support BDS.

While not all hate speech is illegal, political and diplomatic leaders should focus on opposing extremist groups rather than delineating their legal rights, especially in the context of Jews and antisemitism.

According to the International Holocaust Remembrance Alliance (endorsed by the European Parliament and Council), over a hundred antisemitic imagery and language are in use by the BDS.[221] These include cartoons depicting Israel as a hook-nosed religious Jew or as a pig with the Star of David; Comparing Israel to Nazis; Denial of the

Jewish people's rights to self-determination, and more. The report is heavily footnoted, and the examples are accessible online.[222]

BDS's immediate victim isn't Israel but Jews in the diaspora.

A bipartisan US House of Representatives resolution noted that BDS "leads to the intimidation and harassment of Jewish students and others who support Israel." Canadian Prime Minister Justin Trudeau highlighted Jewish students' feelings of "unsafety" on campuses, and a survey by the European Fundamental Rights Agency found similar trends among European Jews.

As the Israeli government report accurately noted, partly because of BDS, "the West has become desensitized to antisemitic discourse when it appears in an anti-Israel context." One example is a recent German court decision ruling that the firebombing of a synagogue in Wuppertal was not antisemitic but merely "a political protest" against Israel.[223]

The BDS movement employs divisive and misleading terms like "apartheid," "genocide," "settler colonialist," and "supremacists" to criticize Israeli actions or policies. This language serves to demonize the Jewish state of Israel and those who support its existence.

The Anti-Defamation League contends that many of the BDS movement's founding goals, which effectively reject or ignore the Jewish people's right to self-determination or would result in the eradication of the world's only Jewish state, are antisemitic.

Moreover, some BDS advocates and campaigns engage in antisemitic rhetoric, including allegations of Jewish power, dual loyalty, and Jewish/Israeli responsibility for unrelated issues and crises. Some openly oppose the existence of the state of Israel altogether or justify or express support for violence against Israelis. Disturbingly, incidents involving BDS advocates holding all Jews accountable for the Israeli government's actions and demanding that Jews renounce Israel.

In conclusion, the Israeli government is far from perfect. Yet, the BDS movement is a modern manifestation of antisemitism, and its true intentions should not be ignored or downplayed. Political and diplomatic leaders must oppose extremist groups and address the impact of BDS on Jewish communities worldwide.

Dual Covenant Theology

By now, you can understand why we, Jews, associate Christianity with most of the persecution our people experienced. This association makes it easy for us, particularly as Israeli Jews, to categorize foreign Christian missionaries negatively and dismiss both them and their message. But this is only one reason why most attempts of Christian ministries to evangelize the Jewish people fail.

Perhaps because of Christian antisemitism, some Christians have taken the opposite approach in response to this dreadful history. Rather than trying to force conversion or turning to violence, some Christians maintain that Jews are better off left alone and without Jesus, arguing that every Jewish individual is saved either due to his Jewishness or by observing the rabbinic traditions. This is often argued from Romans 11:26, a verse we will attend to later.

For example, Pastor John Hagee, the founder and Chairman of Christians United for Israel (CUFI), the largest and wealthiest pro-Israel organization in the world with an estimated annual revenue of $15 million per year,[224] once said in an interview:

> *I'm not trying to convert the Jewish people to the Christian faith. In fact, trying to convert Jews is a waste of time. There is no form of Christian Evangelism that had failed so miserably as evangelizing the Jewish people. Everyone else, whether Buddhist or Bahai, needs to believe in Jesus, but not Jews.*[225]

Hagee is correct in that Jewish Evangelism failed miserably. However, it is a huge logical leap to conclude Jews do not need Jesus.

I believe that what CUFI is doing is praiseworthy and commendable! In fact, many of these Israel-loving Christian believers played a significant role in establishing and growing the State of Israel.[XI] This renewed interest in Jewish roots[XII] and the connection to the Jewish Messiah is a powerful expression of a deeper understanding of the Christian faith. At the same time, as a Jew

---

[XI] For example, the first hospital in the Land of Israel, the first radio station, and the first school where girls were allowed to study were all established by Christians.
[XII] Not to be confused with the "Hebrew Roots" movement, which many consider a cult.

whose life was changed because of Jesus, I find Hagee's words offensive. Separating Jews from their Jewish Messiah is as catastrophic as antisemitism itself.

First and foremost, the primary role of Christians concerning Israel is to "make Israel jealous" (Romans 11:11). You will make us envy you not by grooming our army with more tanks, but when we see you have something we don't – a relationship with our God and a genuine love for all of his creation. Or if I may use the words of another Jewish believer in Jesus:

> *For I want somehow to make the people of*
> *Israel jealous of what you Gentiles have, so I*
> *might save some of them. (Romans 11:14, NLT)*

While financially supporting Israel is commendable, it is not what "blessing Israel" is about. The best way to bless Israel, I believe, is with Yeshua! Therefore, I view "Dual Covenant Theology" as not too far behind antisemitism.

Dual Covenant Theology is a belief that posits two separate covenants between God and humanity: one for Jews and another for Gentiles. According to this view, Jews are bound by the covenant of the Torah, established through Moses, and guided by the laws and rituals of Judaism. In contrast, Gentiles are not bound by the Torah's covenant and are saved through faith in Jesus Christ, as Christianity teaches. While the New Testament hints at God's unique relationship with Jews and their distinct covenant, it is often misunderstood.

Adherents of Dual Covenant Theology seem to overlook the purpose of the covenants God made with Israel. The Abrahamic Covenant is a nationalistic one and unrelated to personal salvation. The Mosaic Law is similarly misinterpreted. The Sinai covenant was about living as a nation under God rather than individual salvation. An individual's salvation has always been based on faith alone, as presented in both the Old and New Testaments,[XIII] and had nothing to do with either the Sinai or Abrahamic covenants.

Moreover, how can someone like Hagee expect Israel to adhere to the Mosaic Law when there is no priesthood, temple, or sacrificial system – all integral aspects of the Law? (These elements were

---

[XIII] This topic is further explored in my other book, "The Gospel of Divine Abuse."

intended as shadows leading to Christ, anyway). But for argument's sake, let's assume salvation could be achieved by keeping the Law and that the sacrificial system wasn't necessary. Could Israel be saved, then?

Repeatedly, the Hebrew Scriptures chastise Israel for neglecting its people, particularly the weak, poor, and needy, which provoked God's wrath. In present-day Israel, one in three children suffers from poverty.[226] Transparency International ranks Israel's corruption rate at a disappointing 60 out of 100. A quarter of Holocaust survivors live in poverty, and Israel is ranked alongside third-world nations in human trafficking reports. The sex trade in our tiny country generates half a billion in revenue annually. At the same time, prostitution remains legal and widely accepted even among Orthodox religious Jews. The International Narcotics Control Board includes Israel among the "countries that are major manufacturers, exporters, importers, and users of narcotic drugs."[227] Israel is a world leader in abortion rates, with an estimated one-fifth of all pregnancies ending in abortion. Since 1948, more babies have been aborted in Israel than the number of children who perished in the Holocaust, as our government funds 20,000 abortions annually. According to BeadChaim, a pro-life ministry in Israel, between 30,000 and 40,000 babies are aborted yearly in Israel, a country with a population of less than ten million. The IDF offers free abortions to its female soldiers. Domestic violence and sexual abuse are also on the rise.[228]

All this indicates that even if salvation were attainable by keeping the Law, Israel is far from achieving it.

Were a prophet to be sent to Israel today by God, their mission would likely be to serve as a reminder of God's wrath.

All Israel will be Saved?

> *I do not want you to be unaware of this mystery, brothers: a partial hardening has come upon Israel, until the fullness of the Gentiles has come in. And in this way **all Israel will be saved**. (Romans 11:25-26)*

The phrase "All Israel will be saved" often triggers debates, particularly among proponents of Dual Covenant Theology. They interpret "all Israel" from Romans 11:26 to mean every Jew throughout history will be granted salvation simply by virtue of being part of the nation of Israel. If we were to accept this interpretation, it would render the evangelization of Jews unnecessary. However, this viewpoint stands in contradiction to the gospel, which declares salvation is attained through faith in Christ. As stated in Acts 4:12: "Salvation is found in no one else, for there is no other name under heaven given to mankind by which we must be saved."

Consider the Passover, when Jews commemorate the Exodus. The statement "all Israel left Egypt" is commonly used. Surely, this doesn't imply that every Jew who ever lived was physically present in Egypt and took part in the Exodus. Rather, it signifies that all the Israelites alive at that moment in time left Egypt. Analogously, when Paul mentions that "all Israel will be saved," he's likely referring to a future event where Israel, as a nation, experiences a profound spiritual revival. It might be a unique historical instance of an entire nation collectively accepting Christ—a fitting miracle for God's chosen people. The pressing question remains, though - when will this transpire?

Two hints towards answering this question exist. The first, "until the fullness of the Gentiles has come in," leaves room for interpretation. As of now, there are approximately 2.4 billion Christians worldwide, in about 40,000 sub denominations, distributed across 7,163 people groups. Whether this represents the "fullness of the Gentiles" is uncertain, but it does suggest we're approaching this threshold. The second hint lies in Jesus's words in Matthew 23:39: "For I tell you, you will not see me again until you say, 'Blessed is he who comes in the name of the Lord.'" In essence, Jesus will not return until the nation of Israel welcomes the one they've rejected. This prophecy, often overlooked by Christians, aligns perfectly with Romans 11.

So, on the one hand, it seems very far. Only 0.05% of Jewish adults here in Israel believe Jesus is their Messiah. On the other hand, "the fullness of the Gentiles" seems pretty close. Perhaps this points to the fact that a slow and gradual increase will not be the case for Israel's salvation but some kind of a national miracle.

In addition to Romans 11 and Matthew 23, consider the "vision of the valley of dry bones" from Ezekiel chapter 37. The vision, found in the Hebrew Bible, depicts the prophet Ezekiel being led by God to a valley filled with dry bones. Then God asks Ezekiel whether the bones can live again. Ezekiel responds that only He knows the answer. God then reveals a vision of the bones coming together, flesh and skin covering them as they come to life into a great army. Then God explains the next stage, which is to bring them into the Land of Israel, followed by the last stage, pouring His Spirit into them. This vision is seen as a metaphor for the restoration of Israel. First physically, then spiritually.

Whether this vision was a direct end-times prophecy or a trend that repeated itself with the people of Israel throughout history is debatable. However, applying it to modern times, we can identify two stages. The first stage is the physical gathering of dry bones in the land, symbolizing the people of Israel returning to their homeland after the Holocaust. This process began 75 years ago with the re-establishment of the state of Israel. In 2013, for the first time in almost 2,000 years, more Jewish people were residing in Israel than in the rest of the world combined. However, even though these bones have been collected and brought back to the land of Israel, spiritually, they remain "dead."

The second stage occurs when God pours out His Spirit. This event resembles a national revival, with the final piece of accepting Christ finally falling into place. This is a cause worth praying for.

Israel's salvation is crucial for the Church, not only because Israel is God's chosen nation but also because it is linked to Christ's return, something every Christian yearns for. However, Israel accepting Christ is a great challenge, as both in Exodus and much later in the Book of Acts, we are being described as "stiff-necked" people!

The phrase "stiff-necked" or "hard-necked" is used in the Bible to describe the Israelites as being resistant or rebellious towards God. This phrase appears several times in the Old Testament, where it is used to describe the Israelites' disobedience and lack of faith.

In the New Testament, the phrase "stiff-necked" is also used to describe the resistant or rebellious nature of the Jewish authorities, who opposed Jesus and his teachings. For example, in Acts 7:51, Stephen refers to the Jewish authorities as "stiff-necked" in his defense before the Sanhedrin.

So, from Exodus to Acts, we have 1,500 years in which we are "stiff-necked." As an Israeli Jew, I assure you, we are still very much a stiff-necked people – so much so that we even killed our own King Messiah and continue rejecting him for two millennia now.

However, this is not merely about Israel; it is about the God of Israel! What do I mean? Growing up, I enjoyed playing various sports games on the computer. As a coach, you could select the most affluent teams with the largest squads and the top players. These teams, such as the Patriots in the NFL, the LA Lakers in the NBA, or Real Madrid in soccer, virtually guaranteed victory in most games and championships without presenting much of a challenge. In such cases, the focus and glory go not to the coach but to the players and the team's substantial budget. Yet, this scenario can be dull, as there is no real challenge.

On the other hand, if you want to demonstrate that you are the world's best coach, you must choose the weakest team with the smallest squad and the most limited budget. Ensure that the players are all stiff-necked individuals. Having a history of enslavement in Egypt can also be helpful. With this team, attempt to win games and championships! It sounds like an impossible task, doesn't it? Well, that is precisely what God – the greatest coach of all – is doing with Israel:

> *For you are a people holy to the LORD your God. The LORD your God has chosen you to be a people for His prized possession out of all peoples on the face of the earth. The LORD did not set His affection on you and choose you because you were more numerous than the other peoples, for you were the fewest of all peoples.*

(Deuteronomy 7:7-8)

While Satan doesn't desire anyone to be saved, his primary concern is not for individuals. Instead, he is focused on using us as pawns in his cosmic chess match against God. Consequently, it is in Satan's best interest to ensure that we, the Jewish people, never come to believe in Jesus as our Messiah. When we eventually welcome Jesus back, it will signify "checkmate" and "game over" for him.

As we have learned, Satan has successfully separated the Jewish people from our Messiah!

From a spiritual perspective, Christian antisemitism seems as if the devil is saying to Israel: "Here Jews, this is what Christ is like! See? I told you you wouldn't want anything to do with this! Christ is bad for you!" Thus, Satan attempts to destroy us Jews not only physically but also spiritually.

As we are about to approach the book's final part, I kindly request that you consider taking a moment to write a short review for the book on Amazon. From experience, I anticipate that some individuals with antisemitic views may attempt to leave negative reviews without even reading the book. Your assistance in counteracting this potential negativity by leaving a quick review would be highly appreciated, as it will help promote and expose the book to Jews and Christians alike!

REASON #3:
WHAT CHRISTIANS TELL US ABOUT OUR GOD

JUDAISM CONTINUES TO REJECT THE GOSPEL BECAUSE IT GOT CONTAMINATED

The last reason for the (ongoing) rejection of the gospel by Judaism is the way some Christians portray God, which often deviates significantly from Jewish understandings, rendering gospel presentations confusing and alien to an informed Jewish audience. As a result, the majority of efforts aimed at evangelizing Jews experience a substantial lack of success.

Israeli Christianity & Jewish Evangelism

Israel is the most Jewish-populated nation in the world, where 74% of its 10 million inhabitants identify as Jewish.[229] As of 2023, Christians comprised only 1.9% of the Israeli population,[230] numbering approximately 185,000. The majority of those are not Jewish nor speak Hebrew natively.

Over three-quarters of the Christians in Israel are Arabs,[231] mostly Greek Orthodox.

Ten Christian denominations are formally recognized under Israel's confessional system: The Armenian Apostolic Church, the Armenian Catholic Church, the Chaldean Catholic Church, the Episcopal Church, the Greek Orthodox Church, the Latin Catholic Church, the Melkite Greek Catholic Church, the Syriac Catholic Church, the Syriac Maronite Church, and the Syriac Orthodox Church. However, the practice of religion is free, with no restrictions on the practice of other denominations.

Hundreds of Israeli Christians have converted from Islam and are mostly part of the Roman Catholic Church.[232] A similar number of Jews converted to traditional churches as well.

Messianic Judaism

The only group in Israel that includes a relatively significant number of Jews who are Christians is called "Messianic Judaism." Despite the Jewish-sounding name, Messianic Judaism is not a Jewish movement. In fact, about half of its members and most of its pastors[1]

---

[1] Over the past 20 years, I was a member of four different messianic churches, all of which are considered large and influential in the movement. Interestingly, all of the lead pastors were non-Israeli Gentiles. The first church was led by a French Pentecostal pastor, the second by an Arab pastor with a Lutheran background, the third by an American Calvinist pastor, and the fourth by an American Southern Baptist pastor. Similarly, my wife attended three churches, all of which also had gentile lead pastors.

are not Jewish.

In 2012, Messianic Judaism in Israel numbered around 15,000 members.[233] In 2022, according to a survey[234] conducted by the Caspari Center, Messianic Judaism in Israel stayed about the same, with 15,323 members. Of these, only "8,125 adults over the age of 18." Additionally, the survey revealed that only 55% of the members of Messianic Judaism have some kind of Jewish background (at least one Jewish grandparent). This means only about 4,500 group members are adults with at least some Jewish background.

The survey also found that out of the 280 churches in the Messianic movement in Israel, only 42% speak Hebrew.

This indicates that within Messianic Judaism, only a couple of thousands are Israeli-born Jews who speak Hebrew, and fewer are of both Jewish fathers and Jewish mothers.

Compared with 2012, and concerning the significant growth of Israel's general population, this indicates a significant *decrease* in members in the messianic movement.

However, from my own experience, most Israeli-born ("Sabra") Jewish believers in Jesus do not attend church services or connect well with the messianic movement but worship on their own or in small groups.

Messianic Judaism is the only group actively evangelizing Jews in Israel in Hebrew, with a yearly budget of tens of millions of dollars.[II] However, these efforts have had little to no success in the number of Jewish converts joining the movement, as evidenced by the negative growth in members.[III]

Having served in ministries doing Jewish Evangelism in Israel for over 15 years, I came to know the messianic movement inside out. I can confidently say that, on average, no more than 10-20 Israeli Jews annually come to acknowledge Jesus as their Messiah. However, we knew how to leverage these testimonies for fundraising, creating the impression of a revival in Israel. Unfortunately, this was never truly the case, as the factual numbers demonstrate.

[II] For example, according to online reports (such as GuideStar), Israel's three largest ministries' yearly budget are about $10-15M each.

[III] Considering the numerous attempts at evangelizing, which have included millions invested in "Jewish evangelism," it is striking to observe a dramatic decrease in the number of members within Messianic Judaism, especially considering that the general population of Israel has nearly doubled within 25 years.

In fact, most Israelis who converted and joined the messianic movement left it soon after to either join other denominations, especially traditional ones, return to Judaism, turn secular, or keep their faith yet disconnect themselves from the messianic movement.

The messianic movement is known for having strong financial ties with evangelical Christians and affiliations with reformed seminaries.[IV]

Messianic Judaism is considered a syncretist form of hyper-fundamentalist evangelical Christianity mixed with Jewish traditions.

Caspri Center described the movement as "Evangelicalism With Some Jewish Cultural."[235]

Theologically speaking, it's extremely hard to define Messianic Judaism. Indeed, for the most part, it's a hyper-fundamentalist form of evangelical Christianity. However, in Israel, the churches are a unique melting pot of Calvinism, Pentecostal and Holiness Pentecostal, Charismatic, Brethren, and Southern Baptist churches mixed with some Jewish practices.

Generally speaking, Messianic Judaism emphasizes holiness, obedience, and moralism. It upholds a puritanical and pietistic ethos shaped by a very conservative old spirit and dogmatic worldviews.

Some members consider themselves "Torah observant" or "Oral Law observant." Some also hold to dispensationalism.

In Israeli society, the Messianic Jewish movement is regarded as a cult both by religious and secular Jews and is not recognized as an official religious denomination by the Israeli government. At the same time, the IDF acknowledges the group's production of devout and obedient soldiers.

Many group members, especially the more conservative, will believe that only fundamentalist evangelicals are truly saved,[V] thereby rejecting and being unwilling to be associated with most other Christian denominations, such as those recognized by the Israeli government.[VI]

[IV] John MacArthur's The Master's Seminary is a popular destination for messianic, followed by DTS, Moody, and others.

[V] Known as "Lordship Salvation."

[VI] As an example, in 2019-2022, a convergence of church leaders within the movement took a concerning course of action, advocating for the informal expulsion of certain Messianic Jewish leaders due to their associations with individuals within traditional Christian denominations. Of course, this is an 'Appeal to Purity' fallacy usually practiced by cults.

As a side note, my wife (Anastasia) and I used to identify ourselves as devote members of Messianic Judaism, as we were the group's most familiar faces and well-known spokespeople in Israel.[VII] However, despite our great affection for many messianic friends, becoming uncomfortable with certain theological doctrines, legalistic worldviews, and other reasons related to the group's ethics[VIII] as well as internal Pharisees-like politics we came to witness, we too became less comfortable identifying ourselves with the messianic movement and simply go by "Jewish believers in Jesus."

Let me share a recent example that illustrates the Puritan-like and hyper-legalistic tendencies I believe exist within the Messianic community. There was a Messianic woman, blind and disabled, who underwent a surgical operation that tragically exacerbated her condition. A complication with her nervous system during the procedure resulted in her experiencing severe, unrelenting pain that even medication couldn't alleviate. After enduring this for a year, with medical experts unable to determine a solution, she lost hope. She chose to end her life at a clinic in Switzerland.

A large Facebook group comprising many members of the Israeli Messianic movement became a battlefield over this woman's decision. When someone posted about her choice and asked for prayer, the thread quickly ignited with a contentious debate. Numerous Messianics publicly condemned her, declaring that if she followed through, she would be damned without forgiveness.

In the face of this, I was the lone voice advocating for a different perspective, one not widely accepted. I urged compassion and empathy, arguing that this situation had no bearing on her salvation. Unfortunately, my stance invited attacks directed at me as well.

As a theologian myself, and one of the only few Jewish-Christian theologians in Israel,[IX] I decided to dedicate this last part of the book

---

[VII] This includes being on national news a few times and having our Hebrew evangelistic videos viewed over 25 million times inside Israel, a country of 10 million people only. We often get recognized in the public as "the Jesus people."

[VIII] We've both seen criminal offenses (such as sexual harassment, which is a criminal offense in Israel) being covered up. Lately, the straw that broke the camel's back was Dasha's murder: https://eitan.bar/dasha

[IX] There are probably less than ten Jewish believers in Israel with a Christian doctorate, most of them reformed (MacArthur's Master Seminary is a popular

to briefly addressing a couple of doctrines that I believe are particularly detrimental to Jews and are a stumbling block in the context of sharing the gospel with Jewish individuals. I believe these doctrines, prevalent in some hyper-fundamentalist evangelical circles as well as in the Messianic movement (at least in Israel), significantly hurt the efforts of sharing the gospel with Jews, making it all the more so a reason for the Jewish people to reject it outright.

I will present these doctrines, and my counter-arguments, by comparing common fundamentalist Christian views and gospel presentations with Judaism's view of God and his character.

---

destination), and of those, I can think of less than five who, like me, are in the field of Bible and Theology.

Christian Misuse of the Torah in Evangelism

Messianic and hyper-fundamentalists often misuse the Torah (the Law) when evangelizing the Jewish people is one reason Jewish Evangelism fails so drastically.

I am sure you came across the viral videos by evangelical Ray Comfort because they are being advertised and have gained about 500 million views on social media platforms. These videos gained popularity primarily due to Comfort's 'Ten Commandments Interview.' In these episodes, Comfort, accompanied by a cameraman, corners unsuspecting strangers on university campuses and in public places to make them confess their violations of the Ten Commandments. Comfort's line of questioning includes prompts like: "Have you ever told a lie?" "Have you ever stolen anything?" "Have you ever looked at a woman with lust?"

If we're completely honest, it's impossible to respond to these queries with a "no." A simple "You look beautiful!" to a bride asking for your opinion on her hideous dress, and you broke a commandment. Taking a pen from the office and forgetting to return it might classify you as a thief. And as for lust, I'm reminded of a situation in one of my doctoral classes in a conservative Christian institution composed entirely of men. At one point, the professor asked, "If any of you here have never fantasized about lesbians, please raise your hand." Faces turned red, but no hands were raised. Be they theologians, pastors, or ministers, we've all been there.

Then, Comfort continues by explaining to his interviewees about God's holiness, "You have to be perfect in God's eyes! Morally perfect!" Says Comfort.[236] Otherwise, "if God judges you according to the Ten Commandments," you are doomed forever in everlasting condemnation "in the lake of fire," concludes Comfort.

Comfort's logic is that because God is holy, he has no choice but to burn you in hell for eternity, even if all you did was still a pen or look at women the wrong way.

On one occasion[237] in August of 2022, Comfort asks a young Israeli-Jewish guy named Ben, "Have you ever looked at a woman with lust?" To Ben's positive reply, Comfort explains that, according to Jesus, it's the same as committing adultery. Therefore, on judgment day, he would be thrown to hell.

The Jewish-Israeli politely rejected Comfort's argument explaining that his views were simply different.

Now, let's take a step back and unpack Comfort's argument.

One of the Commandments Comfort loves using the most says:

> *You shall not commit adultery.*
> *(Exodus 20:14).*

Once Comfort gets young men to admit to looking at women with lust, he then continues onto the following verse:

> *I tell you that anyone who looks at a woman*
> *lustfully has already committed adultery with her*
> *in his heart. (Matthew 5:28).*

There. It's biblically proven. These wicked lawbreakers are on their way to hell. Forever.

Comfort's theological logic operates like this: Any infraction against the Ten Commandments, however minor, merits eternal punishment—being condemned to eternal torment in hell. Essentially, Comfort is telling young, single men: "God has created you with a strong sexual desire inherent to your being. However, if you entertain sexual thoughts for even a moment—and you inevitably will—God will consign you to eternal damnation!"

This line of argument might work with naïve Christian teens but not with Jews.

First, try to apply Comfort's evangelistic reasoning to everyday life. Imagine a world where a police officer could sentence you to a lifetime in prison for parking in a no-parking zone and shoot you in the head if you called him "fool." Or imagine a parent could amputate their child's hand and gouge their eye out if they're caught watching porn. In such a world, the moral standards and ethics would appear harsh and disproportionate, and you would likely perceive something as fundamentally wrong.

And yet, this is the "my yoke is easy, and my burden is light" (Matthew 11:28-30) gospel presentation propagated by hyper-fundamentalists.

For the sake of argument, let's assume that Jesus was indeed attempting to construct a legal case as to why a man (indeed, all men) should be liable for the death penalty (Leviticus 20:10). In that case, just a few verses earlier, Jesus also explains that anyone who becomes angry and calls their friend 'fool' is also doomed (Matthew 5:21-22). So, now both men and women—all of them—are heading towards eternal condemnation once failing at an impossible test.

However, the problem with this line of reasoning doesn't lie with Jesus or the Law but with how fundamentalists misappropriate the Law concerning our eternal destiny. Why? Because, as any Jew knows, the Torah (Genesis through Deuteronomy) never mentions hell or eternal punishment. In fact, the concept of hell was never a topic of discussion among the ancient Israelites.

Jesus simply taught that what you **do** always originates from what you **think**.

What do I mean? Any company that has ever been formed started with an idea, a thought in someone's mind. Any gun that has ever been fired at someone was triggered by a thought (fear or hate) in the shooter's mind. Actions, every single one of them, are first formed in our minds.

If you committed adultery, you first entertained the idea inside your mind. If you cursed, it was because you first got upset. If you murdered someone, you first hated them in your heart. Or, as explained by theologian Andy Woods:

> *Jesus warned you about murder happening in your heart long before physically anything else transpires. Because private thoughts will ultimately lead to public actions. That's why there is so much scripture about us guarding the mind.*[238]

Hyper-fundamentalists tend to read scriptures as a textbook or operating manual written to them. Jews, however, read it very differently.

Although there are laws in the Torah, the genre of the Torah is not judicial but narrative. It's a story - a story that was written in one book, "the book of Moses." Later, the book was divided into five books: Genesis, Exodus, Leviticus, Numbers, and Deuteronomy. The laws and commandments are only a small fraction of the Torah, which is primarily a narrative story. Israeli-Jewish Professor of Bible, Simeon Chavel, explains:

> *The Torah, which contains most of the laws, is not a collection of laws but rather a narrative that tells the history of the Jewish people in their earliest days... therefore we can view the Torah as a source of laws and even construct a set of laws from it. But this is not adequate grounds to interpret the Torah outside of its literary genre, which is a narrative... The fact that the biblical laws are always found in a literary context and not in a legal context means that the laws are indisputably tied to the means and purposes of the literary context in which they are found... The Torah is, first and foremost, a narrative and not a law book, and it needs to be treated accordingly.[239]*

For the Jews, the commandments were never an instruction manual for individuals on "how to get saved from hell" but rather seen as a national constitution. Similarly, no one today looks at the constitution and laws of their country as a means of gaining or losing eternal life. Laws can and will affect your life, perhaps even dramatically, but it's your life in a specific earthly setting. For the children of Israel, the consequences for keeping or not keeping the Law had nothing to do with their eternal destination but with their physical livelihood on this earth:

> *If you fully obey the LORD your God and carefully follow all his commands I give you today...You will be blessed in the city and blessed in the country. The **fruit of your womb** will be blessed, and the **crops** of your land and the young of your **livestock**--the **calves** of your **herds** and the **lambs** of your flocks. Your **basket** and your **kneading** trough will be blessed...The LORD will send a blessing on your **barns** and on everything you put your hand to. The LORD your God will bless you in the **land** he is giving you.*
> *(Deuteronomy 28:1; 3-5; 8-10)*

The Israelites always assumed the God of Israel would save them due to their faith (Genesis 15:6; Habakkuk 2:4), regardless of their works, which affected their daily lives. The "faith vs. works" argument in Christianity is foreign to the Jewish people. Judaism teaches and believes that "All of the Jewish people, even sinners and those who are liable to be executed with a court-imposed death penalty, have a share in the World-to-Come." (Mishnah Sanhedrin 10:1).

The Law was about how to live a blessed life, which is why it never mentioned anything about salvation or heaven and hell. Of course, some laws had a spiritual aspect, yet the Law was Israel's constitution, not "a guide to heaven for dummies."

Israel's ancient constitution, much like modern ones, included taxation (Leviticus 27:30; Deuteronomy 14:28), banking (Exodus 22:25; Deuteronomy 23:19), labor laws (Leviticus 19:13; Deuteronomy 24:14-15), etc.

Maybe if the Torah was given in modern times, we would see rules about not smoking in airplanes and only crossing the road when the pedestrians' light turns green (or white, if you're in America). There are fines and penalties for breaking these laws, but they have nothing to do with your eternal destination.

Now you can understand why attempting to evangelize the Jewish people by telling them that God will cast them into hell because they didn't keep a commandment of the Law makes no sense to them. It's as if I told my son that he was supposed to walk peacefully in the house without shoes on, but since he ran with dirty shoes and stepped on the dog, he is forever banned from the house and is no longer my son!

The house rules exist so the family can enjoy living in the house peacefully and safely. The laws have nothing to do with my son's status as my child or with my love for him. He will always be my child, no matter what. Unless, of course, he chooses otherwise because he doesn't see me as his father anymore. But that's his decision, not mine. For me, he will always be my son, no matter how often he gets the floors dirty. That's what unconditional love is all about. Loving parents are willing to love their children unconditionally despite their imperfections. Why would we think our Father in Heaven would love us any differently?

Likewise, with Israel, the commandments were given so that the people of Israel could live together harmoniously. Of course, if someone broke a commandment, they could face punishment. However, their punishment pertained to their earthly life, not the eternal destination of their souls. Yes, there was a penalty for sin; the penalty could even be death for certain sins. However, these were not spiritual or eternal penalties but physical punishments.

Let's further examine one of Comfort's favorite commandments to quote. The 8th commandment says: "You shall not steal." (Exodus 20:15).

Here in the Middle East, we absolutely love lamb. Say we lived three thousand years ago, and my poor next-door neighbor, craving some delicious lamb meat, stole and BBQed my sheep. So, according to the scriptures, is God going to doom him to eternal condemnation in hell for stealing it (as implied by Comfort)?

Two chapters later, we find out the answer: "If a man steals an ox or a sheep, and kills it or sells it, he shall repay five oxen for an ox, and four sheep for a sheep" (Exodus 22:1).

All we needed was some context to prove Comfort's argument faulty. God will not doom my neighbor to hell for stealing. But he now owes me four sheep, and they better be nice and fattened!

Now, let's make things more complicated. What if a person living in the times of Deuteronomy trespassed two different commandments simultaneously by "stealing" a woman to have sexual intercourse with her. Surely then, his punishment will be eternal condemnation in hell. Right?

Well, no. In that case: "If a man meets a virgin who is not betrothed, and seizes her and lies with her, and they are found, then the man who lay with her shall give to the father of the young woman fifty shekels of silver, and she shall be his wife, because he has violated her. He may not divorce her all his days." (Deuteronomy 22:28-29)

In this situation, that man is to pay the young woman's dad a fine and support her for the rest of her life. It seems you have to pay for your sins, sometimes even for the rest of your life. But this, again, had nothing to do with your eternal destiny.

Lastly, consider King David. He stole someone's wife, committed adultery and murdered her husband, Uriah. In 2nd Samuel chapter 12, when the prophet Nathan confronted David, Nathan spoke nothing about David's salvation. He did, however, announce his penalty. Nathan knew what David knew – his salvation was not in question.

Remarkably, God did not even ask David to resign from office.

Suppose we were to translate all this into modern language. In that case, a Christian may pay a fine or sit in prison for something imprudent they did yet still be saved due to their faith in Christ. The former does not contradict the latter. In Old Testament times, eternal salvation had nothing to do with your works or behavior but with affecting the quality of your life (and, according to the New Testament, your rewards in the afterlife).

The idea that one's deeds are connected to their salvation is foreign to the Hebrew Scriptures and to the Jewish mind and, therefore, will never be a useful method to evangelize the Jewish people.

My intention is not to harass Comfort. I'm sure he's lovely, much like many other fundamentalists I know. Additionally, I appreciate the sincerity and zeal for God that fundamentalists display. However, I believe they misrepresent God's character and the gospel when evangelizing the Jewish people by oversimplifying concepts such as sin, hell, and salvation. Sin is far more complex than God's holiness demanding that I be burned for eternity because I drooled over my neighbor's beautiful new convertible.

For further discussion on Christian doctrines such as the Law, sin, salvation, hell, etc., from a Jewish perspective, please refer to my other book, 'The "Gospel" of Divine Abuse.'

The Gospel Presentation Jews Can't Embrace

The Character of God in Judaism

One of the world's oldest monotheistic religions, Judaism, has a rich theological tradition spanning thousands of years. While Judaism has fallen short in certain areas, such as recognizing our Messiah, the religion still emphasizes God's loving, compassionate, and forgiving nature as a fundamental tenet. These attributes are highlighted throughout Jewish teachings, texts, and prayers, even beyond the Hebrew Bible. This is particularly evident in the fact that Jews call God "Abba" (daddy), a symbol of God's uncompromising love.

During the holiest day of the year, the Day of Atonement, the Jewish liturgy includes prayers such as the "Vidui," "Al Chet," and the Thirteen Attributes of Mercy, which emphasize themes of God's mercy, compassion, love, endless grace and free-forgiveness.

The Shema prayer, which begins with "Hear, O Israel: The Lord is our God, the Lord is One," and continues with the instruction to "love the Lord your God with all your heart, and with all your soul, and with all your might" (Deuteronomy 6:4-5), highlights the importance of love in the believer's relationship with God. The Talmud, a key source of Jewish teachings, emphasizes that God's love for His people is unconditional and everlasting. For instance, in Berakhot 54b, the paternal love of God is illustrated.

Jewish mysticism, known as Kabbalah, seeks to understand the nature of God and includes Chesed (lovingkindness) and Rachamim (compassion) as some of the main attributes of God. The Midrash, a central text in Judaism, uses stories to emphasize God's love, compassion, and forgiveness.

Jewish prayers like the Amidah refer to God as "compassionate and gracious, slow to anger, and abundant in lovingkindness and truth" (see also Psalm 86). The concept of teshuvah (repentance) underscores the belief in a forgiving God who accepts genuine repentance and grants forgiveness.

Unconditional forgiveness is an essential aspect of God's love in Judaism. The Jewish tradition views God as compassionate and forgiving, always willing to pardon. In the Talmud (Yoma 86b),

Rabbi Meir teaches that "Great is repentance, for it brings healing to the world," suggesting that just as God forgives us freely, so should we forgive others freely and repent before them when sinning against them. Of course, God's forgiveness is further demonstrated during the Day of Atonement, when Jews seek forgiveness for their sins through fasting, prayer, and repentance. Leviticus 16:30 states, "For on this day He will forgive you, to purify you, that you be cleansed from all your sins before God." God's desire to forgive and cleanse us from our sins and allow us to begin anew is another striking reminder of His forgiving love.

The medieval Jewish philosopher and sage Maimonides beautifully articulated the concept of grace in his work, "Mishneh Torah," writing, "God is good to all, and His mercy is upon all His works" (Hilchot Teshuvah 3:5). This statement encapsulates the Jewish understanding of God's grace, emphasizing that His love and compassion extend to all His creations, not just the righteous.

Overall, Judaism emphasizes God's loving, compassionate, and forgiving nature, and these attributes are deeply rooted in various Jewish texts, teachings, traditions, and, of course, the Hebrew Bible.

The Character of God and the Cross of Christ in Christianity

Owing to the vast and far-reaching presence of Christianity across the globe, it encompasses a multitude of perspectives and interpretations regarding the essence and core message of the Christian faith, known as "the gospel." The gospel's most essential question is "Why did Jesus have to die?" which met with various answers throughout Christian history. These answers are known as "models of atonement." Atonement refers to how Jesus' death is understood to bring salvation to humanity. Several models of atonement have been developed within Christianity over the centuries. These include the following list:

"Ransom Theory" (aka "Christus Victor"): This is the earliest Christian view of the atonement, and it suggests that Jesus' victory over sin, death, and the powers of evil through his death and resurrection liberates humanity from the bondage of Satan. As Satan held humanity captive, Jesus' life was a ransom paid in exchange for humanity's freedom while maintaining justice (Matthew 20:28; 1 Timothy 2:6). This was the predominance view of atonement for Christianity's first thousand years. In modern times, this view is famously illustrated in C.S. Lewis's "The Lion, the Witch, and the Wardrobe," whereby the Lion (representing Jesus) gives his life to the sorcerer-witch (representing Satan), a sacrifice in exchange for the life of Edmond, the child who rebelled (representing mankind), thereby setting him free from bondage.

"Recapitulation Theory": Developed by Irenaeus in the 2nd century, this model suggests that Jesus' life, death, and resurrection reverse the effects of Adam's sin, recapitulating or "re-doing" the human story. In this view, Jesus is seen as the "new Adam" who brings salvation and restoration to humanity by representing us perfectly.

"Moral Influence Theory": Propagated by Abelard (1079–1142), this view emphasizes Jesus' life and teachings as the perfect example God made for humanity to follow. Abelard believed that the death of Christ was participation in the suffering of his creation to portray the love of God. A love that was willing to die with and for its creation, setting an example for us to follow and live by as well.

These models of atonement[1] each emphasize different aspects of Jesus' life, death, and resurrection and often reflect the theological concerns and cultural contexts of the time and place in which they were developed.

The average Jew (and, from my experience, the average Christian as well) is unfamiliar with these different theories. When evangelized to, the Jewish people mostly heard of the Penal Subtutuiarny model only, which, considering that Jews see God's character so differently, outright rejected it.

"Satisfaction Theory": Developed by Anselm of Canterbury in the 11th century and posits that Jesus' death was necessary to satisfy God's divine justice. Humanity's sins had offended the King's honor, and only Jesus' perfect sacrifice could restore the honor lost and allow the King to forgive without lessening and negating his cosmic respect. Scholars believe this view was influenced by the feudal society of knights and kings in which Anselm lived.[240] It also became the foundation of the "Penal Substitutionary" model that followed it.

---

[1] For further discussion on these models, see Part II in my book: 'The "Gospel" of Divine Abuse.'

"Penal Substitution Theory": Suppose you received a fine for speeding. Unable to pay the penalty because you lacked the funds, your friend stepped in and paid the fine for you. That is the mere essence of penal substitution.

This theory, originating in the Reformation era of the 16th century and championed by figures like Martin Luther and John Calvin, posits that on the cross, Jesus took upon himself the punishment for humanity's sins. As a result, those who believe are no longer subject to punishment. Some modern interpretations of this theory suggest that the torture, punishment, and suffering Jesus suffered were not ultimately caused by men but by divine abuse caused by God's wrath as he violently punished Christ, leading to the separation of the Son from the Trinity.

This view is widely popular in conservative-evangelical, reformed (Calvinistic), Arminian, Pentecostal, and Baptist circles and is also the most prevalent theory held by most members of Messianic Judaism and evangelical ministries in Israel.

Jewish Evangelism: What Gospel Do Most Jews Hear?

Over the last two millenniums, Jews residing in predominantly Christian communities had little to no exposure to any of the above gospel explanations, as evangelism to Jews was mostly non-existing. On rare occasions like that of Martin Luther, whereby Christians did attempt to evangelize Jews, more often than not, the "Satisfaction" and "Penal Substitution" theories of atonement were shared, which the typical Jew found contradicting to his faith and view of God and the Hebrew Scriptures.

Thereby, "Jewish Evangelism" is a modern phenomenon of this and the previous centuries due to Fundamentalist-Evangelicalism's efforts to evangelize the world, Jewish people included.

It's challenging to define Fundamentalist-Evangelicalism from a sociological point of view, but it is an interdenominational movement within Protestant Christianity, especially prevalent in the United States. Its origins are usually traced to 1740, with individuals from various theological streams contributing to its foundation.[11]

---

[11] Including Brethern, Pietism, Puritanism, Quakerism, Calvinists, Presbyterianism and Moravianism. Preeminently, John Wesley and other early Methodists were at the root of sparking this new movement during the First Great Awakening.

According to encyclopedia.com:

> *The two characteristics by which [evangelical] fundamentalists are most easily recognized represent both an engagement with Western culture and a rejection of it. Fundamentalists challenge Western culture in an organized, militant battle over secularizing cultural trends even as they appropriate the latest advances in technology and technique in an evangelistic struggle for human hearts. In an attempt to nurture their constituents, especially their children, within their own subculture, fundamentalists withdraw from Western culture into communities and institutions of their own creation that often parallel the communities and institutions of secular culture.*
> *Both evangelicalism and fundamentalism are complex coalitions reflecting the convergences of a number of traditions.*[241]

Therefore, most fundamentalist evangelicals take great pride in their rigid, strict, ultra-conservative, legalistic, and pious worldview, firmly believing that they serve God through such piety. A good example would be Bill Bothard's IBLP movement,[III] whose teaching is known to have affected millions of fundamentalists in the past 50 years worldwide and at least two million Americans who were directly involved in the movement.

From a theological standpoint, fundamentalism's doctrine of the cross essentially builds upon John Calvin's Penal Substitution Theory (PSA), giving it a modern spin or, as some might say, a "fundamentalist expansion pack." Critics, lacking an official name for this newly adapted theory, have called it names such as "cosmic child abuse" and "divine abuse."[IV]

This modern expansion pack, bearing strong elements of

[III] If you are unfamiliar with IBLP, I highly recommend watching the mini docuseries "Shiny Happy People: Duggar Family Secrets" (Released June 2023)
[IV] Critics of the "cosmic child abuse" expansion are not necessarily opposing the mere concept of penal substitutionary atonement (PSA) in its biblical sense.

Calvinistic-Puritan ideologies, can be traced back to the one many consider to be the father of evangelicalism. Jonathan Edwards was a fusion between Calvinism and Puritanism and played the most pivotal role in the Great Awakening of the 1740s and shaped the face of modern fundamental evangelicalism in America.

On July 8th, 1741, Edwards preached what would become the most famous and influential sermon ever delivered in the history of American Christianity, titled *"Sinners in the Hands of an Angry God."* Here is an excerpt from his speech:

> *The God that holds you over the pit of hell, much as one holds a spider or some loathsome insect over the fire, abhors you, and is dreadfully provoked. His wrath towards you burns like fire; he looks upon you as worthy of nothing else but to be cast into the fire. He is of purer eyes than to bear you in his sight; you are ten thousand times as abominable in his eyes as the most hateful, venomous serpent is in ours.*
>
> *It would be dreadful to suffer this fierceness and wrath of Almighty God one moment; but you must suffer it to all eternity. There will be no end to this exquisite, horrible misery. When you look forward, you shall see along forever a boundless duration before you, which will swallow up your thoughts, and amaze your soul.*
>
> *And you will absolutely despair of ever having any deliverance, any end, any mitigation, any rest at all. You will know certainly that you must wear out long ages, millions of millions of ages in wrestling with this Almighty, merciless vengeance. And then when you have so done, when so many ages have actually been spent by you in this manner, you will know that all is but a point to what remains. So that your punishment will indeed be infinite.*

You decide if this is a picture of God in the image of Edwards or of the God of Jesus. To me, as a Jew, it surely sounds like "Sinners in the Hands of an Abuser." Have a Jewish friend read Edwards's sermon, and he will tell you this is a picture of an angry, hateful entity, not an Abba loving and caring for his creation (Acts 17:28).

Either way, Edwards' views were adopted especially by Evangelicals, Calvinists, Baptists, and a few other Protestant denominations in America, affecting the development of their theological doctrines.

Now, imagine you are Jewish, coming across this YouTube preaching by perhaps the most well-known and influential reformed theologian of our time, R.C. Sproul:

> *We always say the Cliché, "God Hates the sin, but he loves the sinner." That's nonsense! The Bible speaks of Him abhorring us, and that we're loathsome in His sight, and He can't stand to even look at us!*[242]

Or this YouTube sermon, "God Hates the Sin and the Sinner," by reformed pastor Tim Conway, a popular preacher[V] who explains his views of the gospel (remember, in the mind of the Jew, every child deserves to be loved, and as children of God, so are we):

> *All of mankind are children of wrath. We are objects of the hatred of God by nature. We don't deserve His love... God is not unjust to hate mankind. Because mankind is a hateful thing by nature. It ought to be hated.*[243]

Or this statement by Wyatt Graham, a director of The Gospel Coalition,[VI] who defines the gospel in this way:

> *Jesus bore divine wrath at the cross for our sake and so protected us from it. This act implies that God hates humans since he would have poured wrath upon humans if not for the work of Christ's cross.*[244]

Similarly, reformed pastor Mark Driscoll also explained that:

[V] His preaching is promoted through the "I'll Be Honest" platform, with nearly 100 million views on the channel's videos.
[VI] The Gospel Coalition is considered the online hub of Calvinism.

> *God's anger at sin and hatred of sinners
> causes him to pour out his wrath [on Jesus].*[245]

And New York Times bestseller, reformed-Baptist pastor David Platt, explains the gospel in this way:

> *Jesus was pulverized under the weight of
> God's wrath—as he stood in our place...How
> can God show both holy hatred and holy love
> toward sinners at the same time? This is the
> climactic question of the Bible, and the answer is
> the cross. At the cross, God showed the full
> expression of his wrath.*[246]

I do not know firsthand how well-ingrained these views and ideas are within evangelical Christianity in America. However, the few individuals I quoted have online following in the many millions. Also, I do know that most—but not all—members of the Messianic movement in Israel, including its churches and ministries, affirm these views, influencing how they evangelize the Jewish people.

To better help you see it from the Jewish perspective, this is what Jews often hear from evangelical Christians:

> *God gave birth to himself so he could kill
> himself to release his accumulated anger and
> wrath against the humans he hates. This was
> done in order to appease himself so he no longer
> needed to condemn us all to everlasting fiery
> punishment in hell. Why was God so upset with
> us to begin with? Because after he created us —
> as finite and limited beings — we could not
> measure up to his perfect standards. As a result,
> he had no other choice but to punish us eternally
> for not being perfect like him, which is only just.*

Jews often hear a gospel presentation whereby "The angry Christian God so hated the world that he murdered his Son." According to this presentation, not men but rather God the Father inflicted pain, crushed, tortured, and killed Jesus. This gives the Jew an impression of a triune God engaging in a cosmic act of self-destruction or suicide. It presents the Father as an angry and abusive figure who killed His own Son merely to vent and appease his own rage and frustration for not creating humanity as perfect as he is. That's the gospel Jews often hear.

Most messianic churches and evangelical ministries in Israel were established in the last 50 years by non-Israeli, usually not Jewish, evangelical fundamentalists, who imported these views here, shaping Jewish Evangelism.

Consider the following message by an Israeli Jew who endeavors to criticize and mock what he perceives as the Christian gospel. The following is the English translation of his message to me after investigating Christianity:

> *So, what you Christians believe is that God created finite people. But then he hates them and is wrathful towards them because they are not perfect. At some point, he couldn't hold his anger any longer and had to release it. But rather than taking it out on them, he decided instead to abuse and murder his innocent son, who didn't do anything wrong.*
>
> *And this, to you, is "good news" from the "God of love"? If this is the Christian gospel, it sounds distorted and unfair. This is not love nor justice, but an angry, wrathful, and bloodthirsty monster who's angry with himself for creating imperfect creatures!*

Whether advantageous or not, very little information is available in Hebrew concerning the Christian faith. Most of got translated by fundamentalist Calvinistic ministries.[VII]

Imagine a Jewish person googling the question, "What do Christians believe?" or "Who Killed Jesus?" and after reading the answers below, coming to the conclusion that according to Christianity, God murdered himself in a cosmic act of suicide:

[VII] Four out of five messianic/evangelical publishing and educational ministries in Israel translating and printing Christian content in Hebrew are Calvinistic.

"**Who killed Jesus? God. God killed Jesus!**"[247] (John MacArthur) "**Men did not kill Jesus – God did!**" [248] (David Shackelford) "**Yeah, God killed Jesus!**" [249] confirms Voddie Baucham, who was also amazed by the fact that "**God would crush and kill His own Son**" in his place.[250] Likewise, C. J. Mahaney preached to his followers how God "**Crushed his son for you! He crushed Him! He bruised him! He punished him! He disfigured him! He crushed him! With all of the righteous wrath!**"[251] And Paul Washer also says that "**God was going to be hurled upon Him and crush Him to pieces...His own Father crushed Him!**"[252]

Unfortunately, the "good news" preached to Jews often comes across as strange, repulsive, and foreign, leading to its outright rejection. When I first came to faith in Jesus, I found it incredibly challenging to reconcile with these theological beliefs that were widely accepted within the Messianic movement around me. I thought that perhaps I was just not understanding it and that, in time, I would. However, I never did come to terms with it, and I struggled to articulate my objections.

However, 20 years later, I now have the skills and knowledge to recognize and effectively refute its falsehood.[VIII]

Let's examine a few key points within this theology and compare them to the Jewish view.

When Fundamentalism Evangelizes Jews

Two decades ago, I vividly remembered observing numerous young children in the messianic congregations I attended and contemplating the potential growth of the community in Israel to 50 thousand or more members within 20 years. Unfortunately, the opposite has transpired. Considering the rapid growth of Israel's population, the churches have dwindled, and the number of Jewish individuals in the movement has also declined. I have personally witnessed many Jewish Israeli believers in Jesus departing from the church and choosing to maintain their beliefs "from the outside."

It will not be an exaggeration to say that at least 80% of the Israeli Jewish believers in Jesus I grew up with, who were active messianic believers 10-20 years ago, are no longer affiliated with Christianity or

---

[VIII] Since my other book, 'The "Gospel" of Divine Abuse,' was dedicated to refuting this message, I won't delve into it extensively here.

at least have distanced themselves from the messianic movement.

In the past couple of decades, particularly with the advent of the internet, Jews have increasingly encountered presentations of the gospel. During that time, over a hundred million dollars was poured into messianic ministries in an attempt to evangelize the Jews of Israel to Jesus. However, the version of the gospel message that was brought forth through most of these ministries, especially the wealthy ministries, is dominantly fundamentalist and Calvinistic.[IX]

During my involvement in a messianic ministry, we conducted a study revealing that 50 percent of messianic youth in Israel lose their faith before reaching the age of 21. Others have kept their faith but withdrew from the movement. But honestly, I'm uncertain if they ever truly encountered the genuine message of God's love in the first place. I fear that what they were rejecting was a gospel of an angry god accompanied by much legalism many of them experienced.

Since most Hebrew-speaking messianic churches and organizations in Israel lean towards fundamentalism and uphold teachings such as those I quoted earlier, the younger generation finds it challenging to connect with the message. This disconnect results in their gradual disassociation from the community and, in some cases, even from their faith.

Several years ago, I received a message from Dani, a Jewish teenager who had been following my online videos. Dani reached out to inform me about his newfound faith in Jesus, which led to estrangement from his family. Being underage, he couldn't participate in any gatherings.

For a couple of years, we stayed connected through phone conversations until his mother finally consented to his participation in Messianic youth meetings. Dani quickly bonded with the group members. During one of these meetings, he openly confessed his same-sex attraction, seeking prayers and support.

However, the day after his confession, Dani received a phone call from a well-respected pastor based in Jerusalem. The pastor requested that Dani disassociate himself from the group permanently. The abrupt dismissal left Dani shattered. Feeling deeply hurt, he decided to sever ties with the Messianic movement.

[IX] Such ministries include the Israeli Bible Society, Christian publishing houses, most missionary ministries, and the one and only Christian bible college and seminary in Israel, all of which are fundamentalist-Calvinistic.

Despite his decision, I remained his friend and continued to provide him with my support. Unfortunately, Dani's experience is not an isolated case in Israel.

Free Will

In Judaism and the Hebrew Scriptures, free will is a foundational principle. It is seen as a divine gift given by God to humanity. This is highlighted in the Torah with various instances where individuals are seen making choices that have profound consequences. A prime example is in Deuteronomy 30:19, where the Israelites are implored to "choose life" — to actively choose a path in line with God's commandments.

The concept of free will in Judaism underscores the importance of individual responsibility for one's actions and decisions. It's the basis for moral and ethical conduct, as it allows for the choice between good and evil. It is also integral to the Jewish understanding of repentance and atonement; individuals must choose to turn away from wrongdoing and toward righteousness.

The doctrine of free will in Judaism is also critical in understanding the nature of God. It helps explain the existence of evil in a world created by a benevolent God. Humans, with their free will, have the capacity to choose evil, leading to suffering in the world. Therefore, the emphasis on free will is not just an anthropological assertion but also a theological necessity in Judaism.

A few years ago, I was in touch with an ultra-Orthodox Jew from Jerusalem who had come to faith in Jesus. Persecuted by his family and fearing for his life, he had to flee the country. To make a long story short, he got connected with a messianic man, whom we'll call Aspel, who started to disciple him. At some point, Aspel read him some verses and taught him that it wasn't really that he chose to believe in Jesus but that God had chosen it for him, in advance, before he was even born, and thus God had made him believe. He was special!

However, as a Jew, this ultra-Orthodox man was baffled. First, this was a concept foreign to him as a Jew who had studied the Hebrew Scriptures his entire life. But what bothered him even more was the other side of that doctrine. Suppose God had chosen him to go to paradise in advance. In that case, that must mean God had also chosen in advance the rest of his family for everlasting firey torture. "What about my grandmother, my mother, my sisters? Did God choose them for eternal destruction regardless of their own free will?"

Aspel, persistent with his own Calvinistic worldview of

"unconditional election," affirmed this. The idea was too much for the former Orthodox Jew, who felt this portrayed the God of Christianity as unfair and immoral, a God he could not relate to or follow. "God decided to throw my sister and mother into hell because he decided for them they won't believe in Jesus? What kind of God is that?" Following this, he abandoned everything and returned to Jerusalem, rejoining his old Jewish synagogue. By the time I found out about it and tried to get in touch with him, it was already too late. You see, no one had told him this is only one interpretation, Calvinistic views called "Unconditional election" and "double predestination." Instead, it was presented to him as the gospel, backed up by some Bible verses taken entirely out of context.

This experience wasn't exclusive to him. When new Jewish believers start to understand these and other doctrines maintained by the Messianic community,[x] many find themselves unable to reconcile their beliefs and end up leaving. Honestly, I find it difficult to criticize them, as numerous fundamentalist-evangelical doctrines stand in stark contrast to what we, as Jews, understand and believe.

God's Wrath

We live in an age saturated with gruesome action movies, violent computer games, and endless news reports about violent acts. Therefore, it is not surprising that biblical concepts like 'wrath' and 'blood' are often associated with violence, terrorism, war, and suffering.

For that reason, many Christians hearing about God's wrath tend to imagine lightning bolts coming down from the sky to consume God's enemies.

However, that is not the true nature of God's wrath. In the Hebrew Scriptures, whenever Israel would deviate from following God's ways and instead worship other gods, God would withdraw His protection from Israel, leaving them vulnerable and exposed to the spears and swords of their enemies.[xi] This is what God's wrath looked like—a withholding of his protective presence, allowing the consequences of their choices to take effect while becoming passive.

It is as if God was telling Israel, "You don't want me as your boss? Fine, have the pagans and their gods as your boss; see how that goes for

---

[x] For an extended discussion and refutation of Calvinistic doctrines (from a Jewish perspective), see my book: 'The "Gospel" of Divine Abuse: Redeeming the Gospel from Gruesome Popular Preaching of an Abusive and Violent God.'
[xi] For example: Judges 2:14; Judges 3:8; 2 Kings 13:3; Isaiah 42:24-25.

you...." God's wrath was about him becoming passive and not offering his protection to Israel.

As the ultimate representative of Israel —and the entire world— Jesus took our place. He willingly endured humiliation and abuse. He suffered the spears and swords, not of God, but of the pagans (Matthew 26:55; John 19:34; Mark 15:15).

To evangelize Jews that their God humiliated, abused, tortured, and killed the Messiah is repugnant to them.

Sins, Sacrifices, and Forgiveness

Forgiveness of sins and sacrifices are core in all major religions. In Judaism, God's forgiveness never depended on the act of killing an animal. The God of the living does not take pleasure in death (Ezekiel 33:11) because death is the very opposite of what God is: life. Instead, the sacrifices symbolized generosity, dedication, celebration, peace, forgiveness, etc.

So in Judaism, the forgiveness of sins is not about an animal's death, as it is about its blood. Why blood? Because "life is in the blood" (Leviticus 17:11). Blood was like the secret potion of life. "For the life of a creature is in the blood" (Leviticus 11:17) is why the one who "drinks my blood has eternal life" (John 6:54).

For Israel, the sacrificial blood of the Sin Offering was like a spiritual detergent or sanitizer; it could sanctify and cleanse the sins of Israel. In Judaism, Sin Offering was never about death, abuse, or wrath. It was about life and purification.

According to Leviticus, the ritual involved the priest sprinkling the animal's blood on the altar to purify it symbolically. The blood was also used to purify and consecrate various artifacts associated with the Tabernacle.

In contrast to the view held by fundamentalist-evangelical Christianity, Judaism doesn't perceive sacrifices as absorbing suffering and receiving punishment to appease God's wrath on our behalf. In fact, the sacrifices were not killed by God but by the priests, and the death was required to be quick and painless (Leviticus 1:15; 3:8; 5:8). In Judaism, it isn't even about the death of the sacrifice, but rather about its blood, which held the spiritual power to purify and cleanse Israel from sin.

The Hebrew term HATA'AT, often rendered as "Sin Offering" in English, can create confusion for English speakers due to its similarity to the word 'HET,' which translates as "sin." However,

HATA'AT derives from the word 'HITE,' which means "to disinfect, cleanse, purify, or sterilize."[XII] Consequently, in various English translations of the Bible, HATA'AT has been interpreted in two different ways. Sometimes it appears as a "Purification Offering," and at other times as a "Sin Offering."[XIII]

But Hebrew scholars[XIV] will point to the fact that the contextual usage and primary application of this offering in the Law strongly indicate a purification process, as it was utilized to cleanse and purify the altar, the sanctuary, and the various instruments. Blood was regarded as a cleansing agent, akin to a sanitizer or detergent. This explains why the blood of the HATA'AT was sprinkled inside the tent and on the artifacts. This act could be likened to sanitizing an operating room and surgical instruments in a hospital or purifying wounds on the body to prevent infection and promote healing. Similarly, the blood of the HATA'AT served as a purifying agent, cleansing the spiritual contamination incurred by Israel. It had nothing to do with absorbing God's wrath and punishment, as believed by most fundamentalist evangelicals.[XV]

"God Won't Even Look At You!"

In the last 20 years, I was, to some degree, involved with, or at least aware of, most attempts to evangelize Jews in Israel.

Back in my days serving with CRU (Campus Crusade for Christ, an evangelical ministry), the Israeli branch was led by an American Calvinist. We used the perhaps most popular evangelical leaflet ever created in those days. We went to university campuses a few times a week and used this "bulletproof" method to share the gospel. This pamphlet, known as "The Four Spiritual Laws," was written by Bill Bright in the early 1950s. When Bright was in his late 20s to early 30s, he put together a tract to help him evangelize his friends. In it, Bright

---

[XII] For an in-depth explanation, see chapter 3, "Sacrifices," in part I of my book: 'The "Gospel" of Divine Abuse.'

[XIII] For example, the NAB translation translated HATA'AT in Leviticus 4:3 as a "Purification Offering," while the NIV translated it as a "Sin Offering." However, the NIV added the following footnote: "Or Purification Offering; here and throughout this chapter."

[XIV] Such as: Jonathan Grossman, Jacob Milgrom, Yehezkel Kaufmann, Saadia Gaon, Samuel David Luzzatto, and more.

[XV] Based on their interpretation of John Calvin's Penal Substitutionary Atonement model, the reformed view of Christ's atonement.

outlined what he perceived the Christian gospel to be through four "laws." The second "law" states that:

> *Man is sinful and **separated** from God,*
> *so we cannot know Him personally*
> *or experience His love.*[253]

Apparently, our heavenly Father is so furious with us that he won't even talk to us. Yet, he continues to create more of us. According to David Platt, God "could not bear to see your sin."[254] And according to Philip Ryken, God "could not bear to look at the sin" and "had to shield his eyes."[255]

Back in my days with CRU, almost every time I used the Four Spiritual Laws with Israeli Jews, we would get stuck on the second Law. Why so? Because in Israel, we Jews grow up immersed in Old Testament stories through our schooling system and Jewish culture, and these challenge Bright's second "law."

As a sinful human, I can do nothing to earn my salvation through my own efforts. Therefore, salvation is a gift freely offered through faith in Christ. That, however, doesn't mean God hates me because I'm not perfect like he is. The teaching that sinners cannot experience God, that God hates them, or that he cannot even look at people merely because they are not perfect is unbiblical and well contradicted by both the Old and New Testaments.

In fact, the Hebrew Scriptures prove the exact opposite: a holy God who maintains relationships with the worst of sinners.

Noah, Abraham, Moses, and David were all people of faith, yet also great sinners with a very intimate relationship with God. They had a relationship with God thanks to their faith, not because they were perfect. But it doesn't stop with individuals. God loves sinners so much that he decided to even dwell among a nation of sinners. When Jews read their Bible, they see that while Israel constantly sinned, God continuously had his dwelling place amidst them in their impurity:

> *The tent of meeting, which is among them in*
> *the midst of their uncleanness. (Leviticus 16:16).*

In the book of Job, we even read that God welcomed Satan, the father of all sinners (John 8:44), into his company and negotiated with him. Did God cover his own eyes during his conversation with the devil? Clearly, God does not shy away from sinners and can, in fact, look upon and dwell near them. God loves his imperfect children and seeks to draw near them and live among them.

This is especially ironic because one might expect Christians to know this better, given the primary message of the New Testament. If it were true that God cannot look upon us and must be separated from us because of our sins, then the incarnation of Christ would never have been possible.

The central message of the prophets and the New Testament is that God came down to Earth, manifested in the flesh, to pursue sinners and love them. In Jesus, God spent most of his time on earth with sinners and blessed them (Matt 9:10-17, Mark 2:15-22, Luke 5:29-39). Does this sound like a God who is so angry he's unwilling to connect or even look at sinners? On the contrary, God comes near sinners and loves them precisely because they are not perfect! No child is perfect, which is why they need parents to guide, teach, and help them grow and mature. This included the children of Israel (Deuteronomy 14:1) and any other child who ever existed:

> *For in him we live and move and have our being. As some of your own poets have said, "We are his offspring." (Acts 17:28)*

In Jesus, God even "became sin for us" (2 Corinthians 5:21), and His Spirit dwells in us, people who, although justified, still often sin.

How different is this message from the one often evangelized to Jews?

In contrast to an angry, legalistic God who hates sinners and wants nothing but to punch us all in the face and into damnation, Jesus spoke of God as loving, caring, forgiving, full of compassion, and protective Father (Matthew 23:37). A Father who's not only able to look at sinful children but makes an effort to reach out to them, to deliver and save them from their own mistakes.

If you were a parent, would you tell your children you can't look at them or that you must kill them because they are not perfect? If you would never say something like that to your children, then why would you think your Father in heaven would say something like that to you?

It's not that we cannot experience the love of God because we are sinners. On the contrary, it's precisely because we are sinners that we get to experience God's love, grace, and forgiveness. If we weren't sinners, we wouldn't be able to experience, learn and understand what love, grace, or forgiveness truly means. Our sinfulness never prompts God to distance himself from us or withdraw his love. Separation from God is a free-willed choice we make, driven by our lack of belief in God.

This is also what Jesus taught in John 8:24. There, Jesus says, "If you **do not believe** that I am he, you will indeed die in your sins." According to Jesus, our propensity to sin doesn't change. What changes is whether or not we die in our sins. That decision depends on whether we choose to believe or not. Jesus taught something very Jewish: it's all about your faith.

No matter what my child might do, I would never tell him he's no longer my child. He, however, may decide otherwise in case he thinks I'm a bad father or if someone brainwashes him. Likewise, eternal separation from God is our choice to make. God will not impose Himself on us against our will. If we want nothing to do with God, we lead ourselves to a place where he is absent. Essentially, we get what we wish for. No one will find themselves in paradise because they somehow managed to stop sinning, which is impossible anyway (1 John 1:8-10).

However, fundamentalist preachers will point to two verses, taken out of context, to claim otherwise:

> *Your eyes are too pure to look on evil; you cannot tolerate wrongdoing (Habakkuk 1:13).*

> *Your iniquities have separated you from your God (Isaiah 59:2)*

Habakkuk 1:13

In regard to Habakkuk, the key to understanding this complaint of Habakkuk is found in the Hebrew parallelism of the poetry. "To look on" is parallel with "tolerate." Habakkuk points to God's holiness, and essentially, he says, "You are too holy to ignore. No way you can accept this evil in your nation." Or "You are too good to ignore the evil being done." This is *a figure of speech* and not a claim by Habakkuk that literally God's physical eyes can't look at evil.

Isaiah 59:2

When taken entirely out of context, "Your iniquities have separated you from your God" can sound like God is separated from the sinner due to sin. According to Paul Washer, God the Father and God the Son had to experience separation and alienation from one another because God the Father cannot fellowship with sinners. This, according to Paul Washer, is based on Isaiah 59:2:

> *God is morally perfect and separated from all evil. It is impossible for Him to take pleasure in sin or remain in fellowship with those who practice unrighteousness...According to Isaiah 59:2, how does sin affect God's relationship with man?*[256]

Another example comes from the well-known and popular Christian website "GotQuestions," operated by members of the Calvary Chapel movements. The opening statement answering the question "What are the consequences of sin?" reads:

> *Eternal separation from God: "But your iniquities have separated you from your God; your sins have hidden His face from you, so that He will not hear" (Isaiah 59:2).*[257]

What Is Going On In Isaiah 59?

Isaiah 59:2, however, has absolutely nothing to do with "eternal separation from God." Firstly, this is a national rebuke from God, not an individual being scolded. Humans may be separated from God eternally, but not nations. Secondly, the status of individual salvation cannot be drawn theologically from the state of affairs between the nation of Israel and God. Thirdly, the "separation" Isaiah writes about is not eternal but a temporary withdrawal of physical protection and blessings over Israel. Fourthly, the very existence of this verse proves an active conversation takes place between God and Israel. This shows that the "separation" is not a complete cut-off (otherwise, God wouldn't communicate to rebuke). Instead, it is a withdrawal of protection. Fifthly, Israel was a nation of sinners even before Isaiah's time. Yet, they maintained a national relationship with God.

Isaiah, an Israelite himself, wrote, "For I am a man of unclean lips, and I live among a people of unclean lips, and my eyes have seen the

King, the LORD Almighty" (Isaiah 6:5). Not only did Isaiah — a sinner — saw God, but the fact that God communicated through a prophet who admits to being a sinner himself proves the fundamentalist argument to be wrong.

In context, Isaiah 59:2 is about God answering Israel's inquiry as to why His blessings and protection have vanished. Israel has sinned before God, and in response, does God disappear? On the contrary, God is actively pursuing Israel by communicating with her and explaining the consequences of her sins. This is far off from "eternal separation."

Isaiah explains to Israel that her hope for help and protection from evil (Isaiah 59:1) is being denied because she misbehaves. Remember, God already warned Israel in Deuteronomy 28 - if you do not behave, God will not protect you. That is the sense in which Israel is "separated" from God. He is unwilling to rescue and protect Israel from evil.

Thus, Isaiah 59:2 has nothing to do with an individual's spiritual/eternal condition. Isaiah speaks merely about a temporary physical-natural consequence for his nation due to Israel's actions. Isaiah 59:2 means God is holding back his blessings and protection from the nation of Israel due to their bad behavior. If God were to completely cut off Israel, Israel would cease to be His chosen nation. However, God promised Israel, "The Lord your God goes with you; **he will never leave you nor forsake you**" (Deuteronomy 31:6-8).

The fact that fundamentalist preachers have to point to an obscure verse in the Old Testament rather than teaching in the New Testament should also raise an eyebrow.

Now, try to apply Isaiah 59 to parenthood. If your child misbehaves, you will probably reject her request for ice cream until your relationship is mended. You might even send her to her room for an hour. But you will not denounce your child, throwing them out of the house, because they did something stupid. Neither will God, who is much more merciful and loving than you and I will ever be.

The rebuttal I just gave is what Jews already know. That's why "the four spiritual laws" never worked and never will work in Jewish evangelism.

Does God Love or Hate Us?

According to fundamentalism, God hates us all because we all sin. He's furious with us and wants to kill or torture us forever because we are finite and imperfect beings. But fortunately for us, Jesus was kind enough to save us from his cruel Father.

On the one hand, fundamentalism presents God the Father as someone who allegedly hates us and is furious with us. He is unwilling to be in a relationship with us or even look in our direction. He is upset and demands to pour out his accumulated wrath violently upon us, killing us like one kills an insect. In fact, for some fundamentalists, even if you are a Christian, yet you are only "lukewarm," you are still "utterly disgusting to God."[258]

On the other hand, fundamentalism presents God the Son, who is willing to come down and rub elbows with sinners. He is willing to buy sinners coffee and cake. There are even illustrations of him allowing drug addicts to inject needles in his veins instead. He looks at us with compassion, shading tears from the sight of our suffering.[XVI] He teaches about forgiving freely, mercy, and compassion. He loves us so much he is even willing to shed his blood for us.[XVII] The blood that came to put an end to all sacrifices (Hebrews 10:1-18). The Son is pictured as the very opposite of his Father, or at least of how fundamentalists often describe the Father.

Let me illustrate what this might look like to a Jew. It is as if the godhead of fundamentalism extends two hands to us: the right hand represents the Father, who wants to strike us with wrath for being imperfect, while the left hand represents the Son, a gentle hand offering to embrace us despite our imperfections and protect us from the right hand. It's like the classic "good cop, bad cop" scenario we often come across in movies.

But then we're told that as the angry right-hand approaches to strike and kill us or put us in eternal flames, the left hand intervenes and takes the blow from the right hand for us, dying in the process. Finally, the right hand is appeased and can relax. Its wrath was satisfied.

If you think my illustration is exaggerated, then consider the following quotes by these famous fundamentalist preachers.

[XVI] Matthew 9:36; 14:14; 15:32; John 11:31-32,36; Luke 7:13.
[XVII] 1st Timothy 3:16, 1st John 4:2, Phil 2:7.

Wyatt Graham, director of The Gospel Coalition,[XVIII] defines the gospel in this way:

> *Jesus bore divine wrath at the cross for our sake, and so protected us from it. This act implies that God hates humans since he would have poured wrath upon humans...*[259]

Likewise, David Platt, also a famous reformed-Baptist preacher and best-selling author, explains:

> *Jesus was pulverized under the weight of God's wrath—as he stood in our place...How can God show both holy hatred and holy love toward sinners at the same time? This is the climactic question of the Bible, and the answer is the cross. At the cross, God showed the full expression of his wrath.*[260]

And in his sermon, "Jesus sweats blood," Driscoll explained to his church:

> *See, at the cross of Jesus, there is hatred for Jesus and love for us...on the cross, the wrath of God was poured out on the Son of God. To say it another way, Jesus took the cup on the cross and drank every single drop of the wrath of God, and he endured it. This was physical, emotional, spiritual, mental suffering to a degree that is incomprehensible.*[261]

Another famous Calvinist pastor, John MacArthur, wrote:

> *We must remember, however, that sin did not kill Jesus; God did. The suffering servant's death was nothing less than a punishment administered by God for sins others had committed.*[262]
>
> *God put his own Son to death? That is*

[XVIII] TGC is considered by many as the online hub of Calvinism.

> *precisely what Scripture teaches.*[263]

In his sermon titled "The Pleasure of God in Bruising the Son," John Piper preached:

> *Jesus was not swept away by the wrath of uncontrolled men. He was bruised by his Father.*[264]

And in his book, Piper wrote:

> *The ultimate answer to the question, "who crucified Jesus?" is: God did. It is a staggering thought. Jesus was his Son. And the suffering was unsurpassed.*[265]

Wayne Grudem, a Calvinist scholar at Phoenix Seminary, explains his view of the gospel:

> *God the Father, the mighty Creator, the Lord of the universe, poured out on Jesus the fury of his wrath: Jesus became the object of the intense hatred of sin and vengeance against sin which God had patiently stored up since the beginning of the world.*[266]

Another reformed scholar, Dan Wallace, quotes Grudem and adds:

> *At the cross, the fury of all that stored up wrath against sin was unleashed against God's own son.*[267]

Trevin Wax of The Gospel Coalition argues:

> *God killed Jesus. I know that might sound harsh, and it is, indeed, hard to wrap your mind around. But it's true. God the Father sacrificed his Son. He killed his Son in order to spare us His righteous wrath.*[268]

The popular YouTube preacher, Calvinist pastor Paul Washer (John MacArthur's protégé), in his explanation of "how the believer is saved," explains that we are saved:

> *Because of what God did to Jesus: He crushed Him under the full force of His wrath against us...The Father takes the knife, draws back His arm, and slays His Son...*[269]

Nick Batzig, a Calvinist pastor and member of The Gospel Coalition, wrote:

> *Is it right, in any sense whatsoever, to say that the Father was angry with the Son when He punished the Son in our place and for our sin...He made the Son the object of His just displeasure and anger as the representative who stood in our place to atone for our sin and to propitiate God's wrath.*[270]

It is only a small logical step to see how God the Father crushing, torturing, and killing God the Son means that the Triune God committed a cosmic suicide.

As part of a devotional in a popular magazine for Christian women, it indicates exactly that:

> *God tortured His son and Himself to release the bondage and grip of sin on His creation.*[271]

Local evangelistic ministries in Israel translated many of the above preachers' books and materials into Hebrew, indoctrinating the messianic members with these ideas. And when Jews face these statements about an angry and abusive God suffering from a split personality or bipolar disorder, they reject it outright, thinking Christians are crazy. It is not the God of Israel they know about from Judaism and the Hebrew Bible.

A couple of years ago, I attended a home Bible study with a well-known pastor and Bible professor who moved to Israel from the USA years ago. We both attended because a local Jewish lawyer had seen some of my videos and expressed an interest in learning more about Jesus. The idea was to connect him with a local Bible study group, not a church, as we realized long ago that we couldn't direct these seekers to churches because they ran away screaming from the church after a single visit. So instead, we tried to connect them with local home groups where they live.

During the study, the pastor, a genuinely sweet man, shared a story he often used when trying to evangelize his Jewish listeners. He recounted a time when his little girl misbehaved. He took her to her room, told her she deserved corporal punishment, and then began beating himself severely in front of her until she cried out in distress. He then explained to her, "This is what God's love is like. This is what God did for us!" Essentially, he was conveying that God had to punish us for our sins, but instead, God beat himself up.

The pastor had shared this story multiple times, which always made me cringe. Evidently, the Jewish lawyer felt the same cringe, as he never again returned.

Of course, it's an idea the pastor imported with him from the United States, where preachers such as pastor Mark Driscoll say that "God's anger at sin and hatred of sinners causes him to pour out his wrath on Jesus."[272] And pastors like C.J. Mahaney, who preach:

> *Who killed Jesus? The Father. The Father killed the Son. Feel God's love for you revealed in Isaiah 53:10. He crushed his son for you! He crushed Him! He bruised him! He punished him! He disfigured him! He crushed him! With all of the righteous wrath that we deserved. That's what the Father did. So great was His love.*[273]

Once again, pointing to vague Old Testament verses out of context.[XIX] Now imagine you are a Jewish person walking into a church for the first time, then hearing this "gospel presentation" above. You would surely think the God of Christianity is bipolar and abusive, making the rejection of it only easier.

Unfortunately, millions are being poured yearly into Israeli evangelistic ministries and churches to share this "gospel" with Jews.

It's time evangelical ministries and churches —and those standing behind them— trying to evangelize the Jews will realize that these messages would simply never convince Jews to accept Jesus.

Fortunately, these views are not universally held by all Christians. For example, years ago, I had the pleasure of collaborating with one

---

[XIX] Again, I deal with Isaiah 53, as well as other verses used by fundamentalists, in my book, 'The "Gospel" of Divine Abuse.'

of the now widely recognized and loved ministries, "The Bible Project," which produces animated videos about the Bible. Tim Mackie,[xx] the founder and chief theologian of the project, also noted the troubling representation of the gospel I have:

Many of us have inherited a story about animal sacrifice, and it goes something like this:

"The gods are angry with me and are going to kill me. But maybe if I kill this animal and make sure the gods get their pound of flesh, they'll be appeased and happy. Maybe they won't kill me or send a plague on my family. Sure, it's barbaric, but so are the gods..."

Much of popular Christian belief has simply imported a pagan storyline into Leviticus and the stories about Jesus' death on the cross. The result is a tragic irony. What the Bible is portraying as an expression of God's love gets twisted into something dark. Our version goes like this:

"God is holy and perfect. You are not. Therefore, God is angry at you, and hates you even, so he has to kill you. But because he's merciful, he'll let you bring this animal to him and will have the animal killed instead of you. Thankfully, Jesus came to be the one who gets killed by God instead of me. Jesus rescues us from God, so now we can go forever to the happy place after we die and not the bad place."

Is this story recognizable to you? If so, you're not alone. The main problem with this story, to be a bit snarky, is the Bible. More specifically,

---

[xx] The Bible Project, which Dr. Mackie co-founded, received some intense criticism from The Gospel Coalition for not teaching that God hates and that his wrath was poured on Jesus, as posted in their review of the Bible Project ("The Bible Project – Brilliant but Flawed," The Gospel Coalition website; 05/06/2018).

> *the problem is that this story has enough biblical language in it that it can pass for what the Bible actually says about animal sacrifice and Jesus' death. However, when you step back and allow Leviticus and the New Testament to speak for themselves, you can recognize this story as an imposter.*[274]

Much like Mackie, New Testament scholar N.T. Wright shared:

> *As somebody said to me years ago, "If you take a half-truth and make it into the whole truth, it becomes an untruth." And that's a very serious thing because then the vision of God that people have is distorted, and so many people are actually put off the gospel—they just say:*
>
> *"No, that sounds like a bullying God. If there is a God, he can't really be like that."*
>
> *When some people talk about the gospel, you'd think that John 3:16 said: "God so **hated** the world that he **killed** his only Son." Sometimes people say:*
>
> *"That picture is important—wrath and sin and hell and all the rest of it, and it's because God loves us."*
>
> *But simply adding the word "love" onto the end of that story can actually be even worse. It is like what abusers do when they say, "I love you so much"—it's hideous.*[275]

The gospel whereby Jesus saved us from his angry Father by allowing him to torture, crash, abuse, and kill him in order to appease himself is an idea appalling to Jews because it implies a God who is both unloving and ununified. This might be where some rabbis got the "Christians believe in a group of three gods" idea from. Obviously, God is portrayed very differently in Judaism.

The Téleios Family

The "Téleios" family is a family perfectly and eternally united. Téleios household was always perfect in any and every possible way. So perfect, the Téleios family was chosen ahead to be the leaders of its neighborhood. This is due to their unparalleled love and unity as a family. Their leadership was also meant to set an example and model for all other families to admire and be inspired by. In the Téleios household, a father, mother, and son lived together in everlasting and perfect harmony. Their life sets the standard for everyone else around them. In fact, many claim that the Téleios family's unity is the very pillar that holds together the entire neighborhood, especially during times of hardship. The very identity of the neighborhood's people was rooted in the unity and well-being of the Téleios family.

One day, the Téleios' next-door neighbors, the Israelite family, were acting up really badly. They've made such a mess that Fundamenson Téleios, the family's father, finally started getting upset. As they continued with the hassle, Fundamenson Téleios became full of rage, so much so that he had to find an outlet — a way to release his wrath and anger stored up against the Israelite family. However, since Fundamenson Téleios also loved the Israelite family, he took his rage on his innocent son instead. He tied him to a tree outside, pulled out his belt, and beat him up severely until all his wrath and anger were finally satisfied, and he was appeased.

After hearing about such an outrageous event, you, who lived just down the block, had to find out what really happened for yourself. So, you rushed over to pay them a visit, and to your amazement, you discovered that not only was the son indeed beaten up severely by his father Fundamenson, but he was also cast out of the house, having to spend a few cold nights in the streets all beaten up, injured and bleeding. As was explained to you by Fundamenson Téleios, this was the only way he could spare the Israelites.

You left their home puzzled. The next day, you saw a group of people walking up to the Téleios household as they were singing a song of praise: "How great father Téleios' love for us, for he tortured, abused and cast away his son out of his house so he may spare us! For when Téleios the son got severely beaten up, his father's wrath was satisfied!"

Utterly shocked by the ordeal, you picked up the phone, called for a U-Haul, and fled the neighborhood to the city of Secularium.

Will you, as an ex-member of the neighborhood, still consider the Téleios family to be a family perfectly and eternally united in love? Of course not. You would be online filling out a form and submitting it to Child Protective Services.

What kind of logic is it that a good and loving Father would torture and destroy his innocent Son because others were acting up? And if this truly happened in the cosmic realm, what kind of an example does that set for us? Should we also abuse our innocent children when their siblings act up and cause trouble?

I am sure you can understand why Jews reject the gospel as presented to them by most evangelical ministries. They simply can't relate, theologically, to what is being communicated to them. It's not the God they know; instead, it resembles the angry gods of the pagans.

And yet, Christians with a heart for the Jews and Israel worldwide spend millions attempting to convert the Jewish people through these messages. But such a message, barring a few exceptions, will never resonate with Jews - regardless of how much money is spent.

Why Some Evangelical-Fundamentalists Insist God Hates Us?

All major world religions recognize that mankind is sinful, Judaism included. None of us is perfect. We've been born finite and limitled; therefore, we all sin. That's what makes us human. God created human beings with inherent limitations, contributing to our propensity to make mistakes; sin. For instance, our finite knowledge and understanding contrast with God's omniscience. While God knows everything, we often struggle to discern right from wrong, judge righteously, or make the best decisions due to our limited understanding of each situation and its complexities. Additionally, our emotional nature makes us susceptible to manipulation and temptation. It can lead us to act impulsively without considering the long-term consequences of our actions. Our limited physical abilities, such as tiredness, pain, and illness, may also lead to negative feelings toward others, causing us to make wrong decisions or engage in harmful behaviors. These inherent limitations, along with the influence of our immediate environment, past traumas, and personal experiences, contribute a lot to why we make mistakes, commit sins and why we are far from perfect.

Despite this, fundamentalist pastors, such as John MacArthur,[XXI] insist that "God only accepts absolute perfection."[276]

This attitude, however, is quite foreign to the average Jew since Judaism views God as 'our Abba.' I don't know what kind of father John MacArthur had, but in Judaism, a good and loving parent understands that his children are not perfect and accepts them despite their imperfections. A loving parent extends grace to his children as they learn and grow from their mistakes. When children experience grace and forgiveness from others, they learn to extend grace to others who sin against them, thereby fostering a more forgiving and nurturing society.[XXII]

But I don't think the fundamentalist view of God is only contradicted by logic. In the gospels, Jesus freely forgave sinners. He forgave the paralytic man (Matthew 9:1-8; Mark 2:1-12; Luke 5:17-26). He freely forgave a woman known to be a sinner who washed his feet with her tears (Luke 7:36-50) and freely forgave a woman caught in adultery (John 8:1-11). Even when Jesus was humiliated and crucified on the cross, he offered forgiveness to one of the criminals being crucified alongside him (Luke 23:43). Christ chose to use his very last words to express the very heart of God, saying, "Father, forgive them" (Luke 23:32-43). Jesus also freely forgave his disciples after they turned their backs on him (John 20) and then encouraged them to forgive the sins of others (John 20:23) because God always forgives them (Matthew 6:12; Matthew 18:21-22; Luke 6:37; Luke 7:46-48; Eph. 4:32; Col. 3:13;).

Jesus offered God's forgiveness freely before he was crucified. There is a logical conclusion here: God knows we are finite, limited, and imperfect creatures, so he extends forgiveness to us just like any good parent would. However, because God forgives us, we must also forgive others (Matthew 6:14).

Perhaps God Hates Us and Loves Us Both?

If God hates us, yet he abused and tortured his Son instead of tormenting us forever, does this imply that God loves us?

[XXI] Who is very popular in Israel. John MacArthur's Master's Seminary is also a popular destination for Messianic Israelis. Several of his books were translated into Hebrew.

[XXII] I'm not suggesting that criminals shouldn't be incarcerated. However, Jesus made it clear that God's love extends even to prisoners (Matthew 25:31-40).

David Platt was the youngest megachurch pastor, the president of the International Mission Board, and an author of a New York Times bestseller. In a sermon titled "God hates sinners, not just the sin," Platt concluded:

> *So, does God hate the sin and love the sinner? Well... sure... in a sense...But does God hate the sinner as well? Yes! And this is so key to understanding the cross... Sin is the core of who we are in this world. We are sinners with a deep sinful nature and a holy God who is dead set against sin is also dead set against sinners.*[277]

This is what I like to call "theological acrobatics." The logic here, I assume, is that if God hates sin, he also hates sinners. And since none of us is perfect (we all sin), God hates us all. But in addition to hating us, he also loves us, "in a sense," so he is willing to forgive us by torturing and abusing Christ.

I am sure you can see how puzzling this message is to Jews.

Jewish people struggle with understanding how forgiveness equates to torturing and killing the innocent instead of the guilty. If I forgive my son, does that necessitate punishing my dog instead?

Imagine a scenario where Orthodox Jews turned against me, damaging my car and vandalizing my home (that actually happened). Despite being very upset, I still love them. So, how would I reconcile my love for them with my anger? Supposedly, the only way would be to vent my wrath on my innocent son, torturing and killing him.

Suppose I were to present this case to a judge, pleading that I had to demonstrate justice and that this was the only way. I'd likely be sent to a psychiatric institution for life. Yet, for fundamentalists, this argument seems valid.

"Jehovah Rapha" (God Who Heals)

The fundamentalist view of God can also be likened to a physician despising their patients—newborns included—because they have sicknesses. Being upset with their diseases and fearing contamination, the physician feels he can't be anywhere near them. In fact, he must kill or at least torture them forever.

How contradicting is this message from the fact Jesus touched sinners and cured their sicknesses (Mark 6:56)? The gospel is not

"God hates you and must torture or kill you, but lucky for you he tortured and killed someone else instead." The gospel is that God, much like any loving parent, was willing to give his life for your sake. The "red potion," the blood of Christ, cures, purifies, and sanctifies us from our sins. He gave us his life/blood so we can live in him.[XXIII] Sacrificing your life to give life to those you love is what any loving parent and spouse would do. That's the gospel in a nutshell.

I'm not looking to pick a fight with fundamentalists. I am trying to convey why Jews can't and will never be able to resonate with this presentation of the gospel. Yet, this is the portrayal of God that I heard in the Messianic movement in Israel for over 20 years by most churches and ministries. That's the message being evangelized.

This is not a strawman argument. For example, the head of the 'Israeli Evangelism Committee,' who is also a well-known pastor and teacher (of adults and youth alike), a board member of several messianic ministries, and a Calvinist theologian[XXIV] asserts in his evangelistic book written in Hebrew that Jesus not only had to endure torture and abuse by the Father but that as part of that divine punishment and because God allegedly cannot be near sin, Jesus was expelled from the Trinity, "an experience that is the lot of every sinner."[278]

But Doesn't the Hebrew Bible Teaches God Hates Us?

There is a fair question to be asked. How did fundamentalist preachers jump from "God so loved the world" (John 3:16) to "sinners in the hands of an angry God"? Why do they insist that God is "abhorring us and that we're loathsome in His sight."?[279]

It wasn't very hard for me to find the answer, a single verse taken out of context, once again, from the Old Testament.

Marco from Reading, Pennsylvania, wrote to ask reformed Baptist pastor John Piper. The question was answered by Piper in the "Ask Pastor John" podcast: "Pastor John, what do you make of the saying, 'God loves the sinner, but hates the sin?'." John Piper's answered:

[XXIII] In this sense, we "drink" Christ's blood (John 6:54) because life is in the blood.
[XXIV] He was also a theology professor for about 30 years at the only Christian Bible College in Israel. He's not Jewish.

> *It is just not true to give the impression that God doesn't hate sinners by saying, 'he loves the sinner and hates the sin.' He does hate sinners.*[280]

Piper then went on quoting Psalm 5:5-6 to biblically back up his claim.

Likewise, pastor Mark Driscoll preached to his congregation the same motif:

> *The Bible speaks of God not just hating sin but sinners... Psalm 5:5, "You," speaking of God, "hate all evildoers." God doesn't just hate what you do. He hates who you are!*[281]

Likewise, David Platt wrote:

> *Does God hate sinners? Listen closely to Psalm 5:5-6: "The arrogant cannot stand in your presence;* **You hate all who do wrong***. You destroy those who tell lies; bloodthirsty and deceitful men the Lord abhors."*[282]

The logic in quoting Psalm 5:5-6 goes something like this:
1. Those who sin are sinners.
2. Everyone sins.
3. God hates sin.
4. Therefore, God hates everyone.

Practically speaking, fundamentalist preachers believe that every cute newborn, every sweet toddler, and every child playing in your neighborhood's park - God hates them.

On the surface, Psalm 5 contradicts verses like John 3:16, which state that "God so loved the world." (John 3:16). In "world," John is speaking about the people in the world, not the waters and soil. So, what John is saying is, "God so loved the sinners." But in Psalm 5, he hates them? So, which one? How do we reconcile the two? Maybe God does love and hate us both at the same time? Try telling your child that you hate them but love them, and see how baffled they become.

Psalm 5

When interpreting Hebrew Bible scriptures, we must first remember some things. First, unless you are an Israeli, you most likely read a translation in a language other than Hebrew, the language of the Hebrew Bible.

Biblical Hebrew has only so many words, so most Hebrew words have multiple meanings. Also, words change their meaning over time.[xxv]

Second, it is essential to understand the broader context. Hebraist scholar, Mitchell Dahood, explains that Psalm 5 is about the "repudiation of false gods when one was accused of idolatry."[283] Similarly, VanGemeren, Professor Emeritus of Old Testament and Semitic Languages, says Psalm 5 is about God distinguishing himself from other gods:

Whereas other religions brought together good and evil at the level of the gods, God had revealed that evil exists apart from him.[284]

So, with this context in mind, more accurate than "God hates humans" will be to say that God hates idol worshippers.

Remember, the pagans around ancient Israel would not only steal office pens and lie about how nice your dress looks today. They would burn their babies in the fire as a sacrifice for their idols. The pagans were cruel and evil. So, it is them, in this context, that God hates. But this isn't even the main problem with how fundamentalists use Psalm 5:5-6.

The Biblical Meaning of Hate

Much like the term "love," the words "hate" have become heavily loaded with strong emotional connotations in contemporary language. "Hate" is often associated with images of violence, death, and anger. People use "love" and "hate" to express extremely strong emotions (such as when describing their mothers-in-law). However,

---

[xxv] For further explanation, see: "Rule #3: Most Words Have Multiple Meanings" in my book "Read Like a Jew: 8 Rules of Basic Bible Interpretation for the Christian."

"hate" differ in biblical Hebrew.

Unfortunately, preachers often use ancient words translated from foreign languages and apply modern views and feelings. Sometimes they are simply unaware. Other times, they approach the Bible with a clear theological agenda and look for a verse to support their view (eisegesis).

"Hate" = Avoid, Reject, Deny, Ignore

The Hebrew Bible mostly uses 'hate' as a synonym for 'reject' or 'avoid.' The Hebrew word translated to "hate" is SANE. If you don't trust my Hebrew skills, then in the Ancient Hebrew Lexicon of the Bible, 'hate' is explained as something one avoids:

> *The pictograph is a picture of a thorn, then is a picture of seed. Combined, these mean "thorn seed." The thorn, (the seed of a plant with small sharp points) causes one to turn in directions to **avoid** them.*[285]

In Romans 9:10-13, Paul clearly speaks of "hate" in a matter of election. God chose Jacob yet rejected ("hated") Esau. So biblically speaking, to hate someone is to reject or avoid them. To deny your intimacy and blessings from them. If a woman hates her husband, she pushes him away, avoids him, and leaves him. On the other hand, if she still cares for him — loves him — she will argue loudly and get upset with him. You go to battle over the things you cherish most.

Anger doesn't equal hate; apathy does. We get angry when we care. When we hate, we turn indifferent and let go.

This is why Paul says, "No one ever hated their own body, but they feed and care for their body." (Ephesians 5:29). We all know people who hate (emotionally) their body or parts of it. I hated mine when I was a fat kid with zits on my face. But as we just established, biblical hate is not about emotions or feelings of detestation. Paul was saying that no one is **avoiding/rejecting** their body. We indeed eat when we are hungry and don't avoid going to the toilet when our body asks us to — even if we emotionally "hate" how we look or something about our body.

Similarly, we should read "Esau I have hated." It's not that God wished for him a violent and painful death, but God avoided/disregarded Esau, choosing Jacob instead.

Likewise, we should read Psalm 5:5-6. God avoid-reject the idols and those who worship them – these are the evildoers. The evildoers are such because they worshipped these pagan gods and performed the evil rituals involved. God rejected idols because they made Israel do things like burn their babies alive.

The bottom line is that God may "hate" by withdrawing blessings and protection from people, rejecting their appeals, or avoiding them. However, he loves even the greatest of sinners. I know it for a fact - because I am one!

The understanding that to hate means to reject, ignore, or avoid is the only way these words of Jesus would make any sense:

> *If anyone comes to me and does not **hate** father and mother, wife and children, brothers and sisters—yes, even their own life—such a person cannot be my disciple. (Luke 14:26)*

Love would not demand you "hate" (in the modern sense of it) others or your family because that would no longer be love. Besides, Jesus thought we should love everyone, our enemies included. So obviously, "to hate" your father cannot mean hate in the modern sense of despising him. Jesus wanted his disciples to choose him over their families. Not to loathe them.

As a Jew, I had to experience Luke 14:26 when my Jewish mother first found out I believed in Jesus. She demanded I stop believing in him, and I had to **reject** her demand, choosing to follow Christ instead.

To summarize, 'hate' can metaphorically be described the same way darkness or cold can. Just as darkness is the absence of light and cold is the absence of warmth, so is hate. When you reject, avoid, or ignore someone, you hate them. When you don't want to sacrifice for a person, you hate them. God avoided the pagan evildoers, but he loves sinners.

God as a Righteous Judge

Viewing God as a gentle and compassionate Abba doesn't mean Judaism believes in a weak and impotent God. It means we are weak, fragile and powerless. If you hold a butterfly in your hands, you have to be gentle and soft, not because you are weak, but because the butterfly is.

Justice is undoubtedly a concept at every legal system's heart. It is the ideal that all societies strive to achieve in order to maintain fairness and order. However, justice is not always a clear-cut matter of enforcing the letter of the law. At times, it requires judges to take into account the unique circumstances surrounding a case, demonstrating mercy and compassion in their judgments. There is a delicate balance between justice and mercy, and righteous judges can discern when to show grace. A good judge will always seek rehabilitation and restoration of the guilty party in order to build them back up.

Justice is a multifaceted and complex ideal. While the law provides guidelines and rules to help maintain order, it cannot possibly account for every unique circumstance or personal story. This is where the role of judges becomes crucial, as they are tasked with interpreting the law and applying it to the specific details of each case. A righteous judge is one who can look beyond the black-and-white text of the law and consider the broader context of a situation. This, perhaps, is one reason why the Jewish people have an entire library of religious texts trying to cover every possible legal situation, understanding how complex the reality of the law is.

Mercy plays an essential role in the administration of justice. It involves showing compassion, leniency, and understanding in cases where strict adherence to the law may lead to unjust or harsh outcomes. A righteous judge must be able to balance the demands of the law with the need for mercy, ensuring that justice is tempered with humanity.

A righteous judge is one who is guided by a strong moral compass and strives to make fair and compassionate decisions. They recognize that some situations require a deeper understanding and a willingness to show grace. For example, suppose an unemployed single mother steals baby food to feed her starving children. In that case, a righteous judge might consider the extenuating circumstances surrounding her actions. In this case, the judge may choose to show mercy, opting for a more compassionate response instead of the standard punishment for theft.

True righteousness always comes with a degree of compassion and grace. Under the Law of Moses that governed the people of Israel, including Joseph and Mary, stoning was the prescribed punishment for adultery (Leviticus 20:10). Although Joseph initially believed that Mary became pregnant from another man, he made the decision to cover her alleged sin and spare her from disgrace by sending her away in secret. Joseph, still believing that Mary had become pregnant by another man, did not expose her to punishment, guilt, and shame. This is the same Joseph whom the Gospels describe as "righteous" (Matthew 1:19).

To cover for the sins of others is something Jesus learned both from his earthly Jewish father as well as from his heavenly father. As an adult, Jesus' sacrifice on the cross serves as the ultimate act of covering the sins of others. That, while being abused and murdered by the wicked man-made system that punishes the Righteous while setting the real criminals free. God didn't kill the Righteous one. We did.

Joseph's actions point to the very nature of God as a merciful judge toward sinners. When we do fall, God does not seek to cast stones at us. Instead, he covers our sins and offers us hope and the promise of eternal life.

Just like in the case of Joseph, discretion is a crucial tool for righteous judges, allowing them to make case-by-case decisions that consider each situation's unique circumstances. When judges exercise discretion wisely, they can ensure that justice is served in a manner that acknowledges the complexities of human nature and the nuances of individual cases. This flexibility is vital in maintaining a fair and just legal system.

In conclusion, Justice is not a one-size-fits-all concept, and its implementation requires a delicate balance between upholding the law and showing grace and compassion when appropriate. Righteous judges play a critical role in ensuring that our legal system remains fair, compassionate, and just. By exercising their discretion and considering the broader context of each case, these judges can make decisions that take into account the complexities of human nature and the unique circumstances of each situation. In doing so, they uphold the true spirit of justice, demonstrating that mercy and compassion are essential components of a just legal system.

Regardless of how good, righteous, and compassionate a human judge may be, God exceeds this a million times over.

The Loving Jewish Father

So, what gospel message then should be evangelized to Jews?

When contemplating the nature of God's love, I am invariably drawn to the unconditional love that parents ideally bestow upon their children. This profound affection is not a reward for merit but rather an innate and unwavering connection between parent and child. God is our Father, and we are his cherished children. This divine love transcends our accomplishments and shortcomings, enveloping us in its tender embrace regardless of our triumphs and tribulations.

God's love for us is not based on whether we deserve it. God loves us just as parents love their children unconditionally, regardless of their imperfections and mistakes.

So what gospel message do I believe Jews need to hear? How should we describe God to be? It only make sense that we have to go back and share with Jews exactly what Jesus shared with them.

The Parable of the Prodigal Son, found in Luke 15:11-32, tells the story of a younger Jewish son who demands his inheritance from his Jewish father, then squanders it all in a far-off country, living a life of reckless indulgence. After facing destitution and famine, the son comes to his senses. Realizing his wrongdoing, the younger brother decided to change his path and return home. That's what true repentance is all about.

However, because the prodigal son offended and humiliated his father, he decided to tell him: "I am no longer worthy to be called your son!" The son mistakenly thought his father won't or shouldn't love him because of this behavior. His sins, so the son thought, made him unworthy of his father's love (which is precisely what so many Christians today preach).

However, his father proved him wrong "he ran to his son, threw his arms around him and kissed him." This happened before the son even apologized! Kids run and play; fathers do not. In the Middle Eastern culture of those days, it was way beneath the honor of a patriarch to run like a small child. They sit and wait as you come to show them respect. But here, the father is the one running to the son who has humiliated and sinned against him. That's unheard of! But this father was like no other. He loves his children despite their sins. His heart is broken for them.

But even before this happened, "his father saw him from far away." This must mean the father was waiting outside the house for his son in the heat and rain, desperately longing for the day he might return.

Now, while the father had every right to be angry, without anyone blaming him if he decided to "pour his wrath" on his son by stoning him to death as the Law permits (Deuteronomy 21:18-21), he did not. Against all odds, against any religious logic, and against what must have "felt right" for Jesus's audience, not only was the father not upset with his son, but he also ran, kissed, and hugged his young son.

The son did not shake his dad's hand (western culture) or bow in respect (eastern culture). Instead, the father kissed and hugged him as if to say, "You are family. Welcome back home. I missed you."

The conservative Pharisees who heard this parable probably expected the father to at least tell his returning son something like:

> *Young man, you stink from pigs. You know how we feel about pigs in this Jewish house. Go, clean yourself up, and then come back so we can discuss your actions to earn back the status you have lost because of your foolish behavior. And, if I see that you get your act together, I might consider you a son again. Servants, quick! Bring a Bible and put it in his hands!*

However, that wasn't the case with this father, who could not bear to see his son barefoot and in filth for one more second. Not only did the father refuse to let his young son become a servant, but he would barely even let him say his apology! In fact, the father ran to his son and hugged him before the son even spoke a word! It was much easier for the son to ask for forgiveness once he was hugged and kissed by his father, proving he loved his son regardless of his sins. This is a good lesson for us as well. Forgive freely regardless of someone's willingness to repent.

This parable Jesus told went against the very fundamental teaching of the Pharisees (of all kinds and eras) as it shows that God is not seeking to punish, take revenge, and outcast sinners, but to forgive, cover their shame, and assure them of their spiritual status as children of God!

That was the message of the Jewish Messiah to the Jewish people. That should also be the message Jews hear from Christians today!

When I think about God's love, I am reminded that my worth is not dependent on my achievements, my failures, or how others perceive me. My worth is inherent because I am a child of God, and God's love for me is constant and unchanging. Believing the idea that "I don't deserve God's love" is a disservice to the profound nature of God's love, which is both unconditional and transformative. Fear turns sinners into legalist. Love helps them change, mature and grow.

Embracing the truth of God's unconditional love allows me to grow in my relationship with God and extend that love to others. It empowers me to forgive myself and others, to show compassion and empathy, and to strive for growth and positive change.

God does not harbor hatred for sinners or desire to condemn them solely based on their sins. Instead, he intends to heal, mend, and rejuvenate their souls, a transformative journey that will culminate when we are granted new and resurrected bodies (1 Corinthians 15).

Amen.

Epilogue

As a Jew, when I initially came to believe that Jesus was my Messiah, I felt it was impossible for me to share with family and friends that I believe Jesus is my Messiah. It took my mother a couple of years to understand my conviction, and when she did, her reaction was one of fury. Despite her not being religious, we didn't speak for a long time (thankfully, we now enjoy a great relationship.)

For Jews from traditional or religious backgrounds, embracing Jesus can be even more challenging. Such a decision can evoke various negative responses within their Jewish communities. The reactions can vary depending on the individual, family, and community. Common negative responses may include ostracization from family, friends, and community, which can lead to emotional isolation.

In more close-knit communities, converted individuals may face boycotts of their businesses or services, leading to significant financial strain. They might also find themselves excluded from social events, religious gatherings, or community activities, exacerbating feelings of isolation and alienation. Some individuals may face public criticism or shaming, damaging their reputation within the community. In some cases, these individuals might even face physical persecution and property damage by the orthodox Jews, as I have often experienced.

They may also face extreme pressure to reconsider their decision, with family and community members trying to persuade them to return to rabbinic Judaism, often employing coercion, threats, and manipulation. Some orthodox Jewish communities may even perform a funeral ceremony for the converted individual, symbolically mourning their "death," a gesture that can be emotionally traumatic.

These experiences aren't universal, and their severity can vary widely. More liberal Jewish communities may be more accepting, while others may be more resistant.

Given our history of persecution, Jewish communities emphasize the importance of unity, making the experience of ostracization for Jewish believers in Jesus particularly traumatic.

By now, you should have a clearer understanding not just of the primary reasons Jews reject Jesus but you have also gained insight into the complexities that Jews face in accepting Jesus.

However, in my personal journey, I have discovered that Christian believers in Jesus can fill the social void left in our hearts. Therefore, Christians must make us, Jewish believers in Jesus, feel loved and included in the family.

Regarding evangelism, I'm well aware that many Christians with a warm heart for Israel and the Jewish people have attempted to evangelize us, mostly with limited success. As you have now come to appreciate, we have much to lose.

As Jews, we are known for our intellect and appreciate well-reasoned explanations and debates. And while there are resources available to help you with this, including my own book, "Refuting Rabbinic Objections to Christianity," it's essential that you first establish a foundation of trust with your Jewish friends before diving into theological discussions. Trusting a Christian will not likely come easy to a Jew; therefore, trust is the foundation of Jewish evangelism, prioritizing relationship-building. So, regarding Jewish evangelism, consider extending an invitation to share a meal before presenting a pamphlet.

Lastly, I'd like to ask a personal favor. Given the nature of my work, antisemites may leave negative reviews and rate my book negatively, and I speak of experience. This can sometimes also be true regarding Orthodox Jews. Therefore, if my book has been a blessing to you, I kindly request you take a few seconds and leave a short review (or at least a rating) on Amazon. I read all your reviews!

Thank you in advance! I really do appreciate it!
Dr. Eitan Bar.

P.S. You may stay in touch through my website: www.eitan.bar

Other books by Dr. Eitan Bar include:

- The "Gospel" of Divine Abuse: Redeeming the Gospel from Gruesome Popular Preaching of an Abusive and Violent God.
- Read Like a Jew: 8 Rules of Basic Bible Interpretation for the Christian.
- Refuting Rabbinic Objections to Christianity & Messianic Prophecies.
- Rabbinic Judaism Debunked: Debunking the myth of Rabbinic Oral Law (Oral Torah).
- Spiritual Nuggets: 30 Devotions Filled with Grace and Hope for the Weary and Hurting.
- Reading Moses, Seeing Jesus: How the Torah (Law) Fulfills its Goal in Yeshua (Jesus).

Photo books:

- The Jerusalem Coffee Table Photobook: Extraordinary monochromatic photography of Jerusalem joined with Bible verses
- The Israel Coffee Table Photobook: Most exceptional photography of Israel's famous sceneries

Endnotes

[1] Mark Twain, September 1897 (Quoted in *The National Jewish Post & Observer*, June 6, 1984
[2] https://www.nytimes.com/2010/01/12/opinion/12brooks.html
[3] Spurgeon, "The Restoration and Conversion of the Jews," MTP, 10:426.
[4] Mordechai Altshuler, Judaism in the Soviet Oppression: Between Religion and Jewish Identity in the Soviet Union 1964-1941, Jerusalem, Zalman Shazar Center for the Study of the History of the Jewish People, 2008, p. 391
[5] Avraham Melamed, Religion: From Law to Belief - The History of a Designated Nomenclature, published by: The United Kibbutz, 2014, p.16
[6] Ibid. p. 220.
[7] Daniel Boyarin, The Jewish Gospels, The New Press, 2012, see in the Introduction.
[8] www.daat.ac.il/he-il/hagim/hodashim/yom_hakipurim/stav-lashon.htm
[9] David Hartman, Love and Fear in the Encounter with God: The Theological Legacy of Rabbi Yosef Dov Soloveitchik, published by Shalom Hartman Institute, 2006, pp. 103-105.
[10] Yaakov Katz, Between Jews and Gentiles, published by: Mossad Bialik, Jerusalem, 1961, p. 143.
[11] Gili Zivan, Religion Without Illusion: Facing a Postmodernist World, Ra'anana, published by: The United Kibbutz Shalom Hartman Institute, Bar-Ilan University, Faculty of Law, 2005, p. 207.
[12] :Or as Jacob Neusner calls it, "Theology of the Oral Torah", in Jacob Neusner , The Four Stages of Rabbinic Judaism, Taylor & Francis, 2002, p.
[13] Ephraim Shmueli, The "Essence" of Judaism and the "Identity" of the Jew in terms of our time, Mazeniz, Book of the Jubilee, 1979, pp. 325-333.
[14] Israel L. Levin (editor), Continuity and Permutation: Jews and Judaism in the Byzantine-Christian Land of Israel, Jerusalem, published by: Yad Yitzhak Ben-Zvi Dinor Center for the Study of Israel's History, 2004, pp. 302-303.
[15] Menachem Kellner, Faith that does not reach the point: How is Judaism tested, Jerusalem, Shalem Publishing, 2016, p. 76.
[16] Ibid., p. 30.
[17] Ibid., p. 32.
[18] Israel Jacob Yuval, The Passover Haggadah on the Two Sections: The Passover Haggadah and the Christian Passover, Tarvitz, Volume 66, Booklet 1, 5566, pp. 5-28.
[19] Avraham Melamed, Religion: From Law to Belief - The History of a Defined Nomenclature, published by: Kibbutz Ha'Echad, 2014, pp. 36-37, 296-297 ; And also: Roy A. Stewart, Rabbinic theology: An introductory study, Oliver and Boyd, 1961.
[20] Israel Jacob Yuval named his book, "Two Nations in Your Womb: Perceptions of Jews and Christians in Late Antiquity and the Middle Ages" (University of California Press, 2008.)
[21] Dov Rafel, Methodological and programmatic notes for the study of Jewish educational thought, Proceedings of the World Congress for Jewish Studies, III: Talmud and Midrash, Philosophy and Kabbalah, Hebrew Literature, World Association for Jewish Studies, 1981, pp. 117-121.
[22] Israel Dov Albaim (creator and editor), The Declaration of Independence with an Israeli Talmud, published by: Yedioth Ahronoth Sefri Hamad, 2019, p. 119.
[23] Israel Bartel, Yeremiahu Yuval, Yair Tsavan, David Shachem and Menachem Rickner (editors), A New Jewish Time: Jewish Culture in a Secular Age, Volume One, Crown Publishing for Lamda - Association for Modern Jewish Culture, 2007, p. 206.
[24] Menachem Kellner, ibid., p. 53.
[25] Shlomo Fisher, in: Shlomo Fisher and Adam B. Seligman (editors), The yoke of tolerance: religious traditions and the challenge of pluralism, published by: Van Leer Institute in Jerusalem, the United Kibbutz, 2007, p. 179.
[26] Adiel Shermer, in: Israel Bartel, Yeremiahu Yuval, Yair Tsavan, David Shaham and Menachem Brinker (editors), A New Jewish Time: Jewish Culture in a Secular Era - An Encyclopedic View - Volume One: Modern Jewish Thought; memory, myth and history; Changes in lifestyles, Keter publishing house for Mada - Association for Modern Jewish Culture AR, 2007, p.

206.

[27] Dov Rafel, Methodological and programmatic notes for the study of Jewish educational thought, Proceedings of the World Congress of Jewish Studies, III: Talmud and Midrash, Philosophy and Kabbalah, Hebrew Literature, World Association for Jewish Studies, 1981, pp. 121-171.

[28] 8.5.2012 ,"ידיעות אחרונות, מוסף יהדות, "למה צריך את התורה שבעל פה

[29] משה בן דוד, על פתחה של רומי, הוצאה עצמאית, עמ' 479.

[30] Introduction to H. Chaim Schimmel, *The Oral Law: A Study of the Rabbinic Contribution to Torah She-be-al-Peh* (2nd, rev. ed.; Jerusalem/New York: Feldheim, 1996), n.p.

[31] www.youtube.com/watch?v=9Li8YbeN2OE

[32] Gittin 56b and 57a

[33] Yomma 28b.

[34] Midrash Tanna Debei Eliyahu, Chapter 6, p. 65; Leviticus Raba says that Jacob, Judah and Joseph fulfilled "what is written in the Torah" (Parasha B10) and that Jacob sat in two schools (Genesis Raba, Toldot 10); Moses had a Beth Midrash of his own (Yerushalmi Eruvin 32b; Chapter 5, Oral Law 1); Joshua Bin Nun was chastised by an angel of God for daring to go to war and thus setting aside the study of Torah (Bavli, Megilla 3a); and King David, as he studied in a Yeshiva, "He would not sit upon pillows and cushions. Rather, he would sit on the ground" and "When David would sit and occupy himself with Torah, he would make himself soft as a worm, and when he would go out to war, he would make himself hard and strong as a tree" (Moed Katan 16b). By the way, Our Sages also believed that "The first man, Adam, knew the Torah and handed it down to his son Seth, followed by Hanoch, until it was given to Shem, who was busy with it" (Rabbi Meir Ben Gabbi, Avodat HaKodesh, Part 3, Chapter 21). Even relating to Betzalel Ben Uri it was said that "the spirit of God filled him with wisdom – as he was a Torah scholar, with intelligence – as he understood the Oral Law, and with knowledge – as his mind was filled with the Talmud" (Midrash Tanchuma, Exodus, Vayekahel, Chapter 5).

[35] Avodah Zarah 3b; and Midrash Eliyahu Zuta, Chapter 20.

[36] Midrash Tanna Debei Eliyahu, Chapter 3, p. 25

[37] Yerushalmi, Berakhot 8b.

[38] Pessachim 22b. They must be greatly feared as for "their bite is the bite of a fox, their sting is the sting of a scorpion, their hiss is the hiss a serpent, and all their words are like fiery coals" (Mishnah, Avot 2:13).

[39] As written: "Awe of your rabbi is like awe of the heavens" (ibid, 4:15).

[40] מדריך לתלמוד , עדין שטיינזלץ, 2002:26. The waning status of the Priests is evident from the Talmudic phrase: "If a wise student was a bastard and a great Priest an ignoramus, the bastard wise student shall precede the ignoramus Priest" (Yerushalmi, Horayot 18b, Chapter 3, Oral Law 5; Bavli, Horayot 13a). For rabbis, the Oral Law is "Greater is learning Torah than the priesthood and than royalty" (Mishnah, Avot 6:6).

[41] These relations were also maintained in the Middle Ages, as evident in the words of Maimonides: "There is no greater respect than that granted the rabbi (Mishneh Torah, Talmud Torah Laws, Chapter 5b)

[42] Yevamot 20a

[43] Avot 1:4

[44] Eruvin 21b.

[45] Gittin 57a

[46] Talmud, Bava Metzia 59b.

[47] Talmud, Bava Metzia 59b.

[48] Talmud, Bava Metzia 59b.

[49] Talmud, Bava Metzia 59b.

[50] Halachot Mamrim, Chapter 3, Paragraph 1

[51] יורם ארדר, הקרע בין העדה הרבנית לעדה הקראית בתקופת הגאונים, ציון, החברה ההיסטורית הישראלית, תשע"ג, עמ' 321-349

[52] נ' ה' טור-סיני, הלשון והספר: בעיות יסוד במדע הלשון ובמקורותיה הספרותיים – כרך הספר, מוסד ביאליק, 1959, עמ' 391. In practice, the rabbis considered themselves kings and actually demanded to be treated as such. See עדין שטיינזלץ, מדריך לתלמוד, הוצאת כתר, 2002, עמ' 24

[53] Pessachim 22b; 108a.

[54] Yerushalmi Talmud, Berakhot 8b

[55] Bava Batra 12a
[56] Eruvin 21b
[57] Herbert Henry Asquith, Letters of the Earl of Oxford and Asquith to a Friend, Vol. 2 (1933), p. 94.
[58] Stephen Wylen, The Jews in the Time of Jesus: An Introduction, Mahwah, Paulit Press, (1995), page 190.
[59] N. T. Wright, The New Testament and the People of God, Minneapoli, Fortress Press, (1992), pp. 164–165.
[60] https://lib.toldot.cet.ac.il/pages/item.asp?item=18026
[61] אביגדור שנאן, פרקי אבות: פירוש ישראלי חדש, ידיעות אחרונות, ספרי חמד, ירושלים, 2009, עמ' 12.
[62] https://he.chabad.org/library/article_cdo/aid/504544/jewish/-.htm
[63] Sanhedrin 96b in Yad HaRav Herzog manuscript (text: מבני בניו של סיסרא לימדו תורה בירושלם ומנו ר' עקיבה) but not other manuscripts; Nissim Gaon, commentary to Brachot 27b, quoting Sanhedrin 96b; Maimonides, commentary to the Mishna, introduction; Yalkut Reuveni, Vayeshev
[64] ערן קמחי, שחרור המקום: דרך למהגר בעולם, 2016: 123-124.
[65] https://www.timesofisrael.com/new-shas-mk-has-said-immodest-women-get-breast-cancer-reincarnate-as-cows/
[66] משנה תורה, הלכות תפילין ומזוזה וספר תורה, פרק ה.
[67] צבי מרק, מיסטיקה ושיגעון ביצירת ר' נחמן מברסלב, 2003: 59-61.
[68] קונג פו-צה" (עורך: מ' מ' בובר), מאמרות, מוסד ביאליק, 1960: 36".
[69] משה פלאי, עטרה ליושנה: המאבק ליצירת יהדות ההשכלה, 2012: 66, 182.
[70] https://www.ynet.co.il/articles/0,7340,L-4886218,00.html
[71] קיצור שולחן ערוך, קכח יג.
[72] רחל אלאור, מקומות שמורים: מגדר ואתניות במחזיות הדת והתשובה, הוצאת עם עובד, 2006: 41-59.
[73] משה פלאי, עטרה ליושנה: המאבק ליצירת יהדות ההשכלה, 2012: 66-67.
[74] https://oral.law/%d7%aa%d7%a4%d7%99%d7%9c%d7%94/
[75] https://www.chabad.org/library/article_cdo/aid/42944/jewish/Lag-BaOmer.htm
[76] "Love and Anger at the Cross?" reformation21, January 6, 2019
[77] Driscoll, "Jesus Sweats Blood," realfaith, July 4, 2016
[78] Anyabwile, What Does It Mean for the Father to Forsake the Son?
[79] Living Better 50 Magazine, April 14, 2021 devotional
[80] https://www.hidabroot.org/article/78994
[81] Kaniel, "Sacredness and Sanctity", pg. 43.
[82] Zohar Part 3:1; in Hebrew by Rabbi Zvi Nashi, "Harez Desholsha".
[83] https://meirtv.com/alon-1500/
[84] Eikhah Rabbah 3
[85] Limor, Between Jews and Christians, pg. 83.
[86] Daniel Boyarin, The Jewish Gospels: The Story of the Jewish Christ (2011), pg. 5
[87] Daniel Boyarin, The Jewish Gospels: The Story of the Jewish Christ (2011), pg. 6
[88] https://jesusplusnothing.com/series/post/jesusbringasword
[89] https://youtu.be/w3Ucx8tdNVE
[90] https://www.knowingfaith.co.il/%D7%99%D7%A1%D7%95%D7%93%D7%95%D7%AA-%D7%94%D7%90%D7%9E%D7%95%D7%A0%D7%94/%D7%93%D7%A2-%D7%9E%D7%94-%D7%A9%D7%AA%D7%A9%D7%99%D7%91-%D7%9C%D7%9E%D7%99%D7%A1%D7%99%D7%95%D7%A0%D7%A8
[91] McGuckin, John Anthony (2004). "The Life of Origen (ca. 186–255)".
[92] California State University at Northridge, "Canons of the Church Council at Elvira (Granada) ca. 309 AD," www.csun.edu/~hcfll004/elvira.html
[93] Gonzalez, Justo L. (2010-08-10). The Story of Christianity: Volume 1: The Early Church to the Dawn of the Reformation. Zondervan. pp. 149–150.
[94] Centre for the Study of Historical Christian Antisemitism, "John Chrysostom," www.hcacentre.org/JohnChrysostom.html
[95] Justin Martyr, "Dialogue with Tryphon" (Hebrew translation), Magnes, 2004. Chapter 135.
[96] Such as the Tanhuma Midrash Vayyera 5:3
[97] Michael Avi-Yona, In the days of Rome and Byzantium, Bialik Institute, Jerusalem, 1980, p. 148 (my emphasis).

[98] "Faith and Fratricide: The Theological Roots of Anti-Semitism" by Rosemary Radford Ruether (1974).
[99] The Origins of Anti-Semitism: Attitudes Toward Judaism in Pagan and Christian Antiquity" by John G. Gager (1983).
[100] "Holy Hatred: Christianity, Antisemitism, and the Holocaust" by Robert Michael (2006).
[101] Asor, *Al Pitcha Shel Rome*, pg. 22.
[102] Fruchtenbaum, *Israelology*, 405.
[103] Lenski, The Interpretation of Saint Paul's Epistles to the Galatians , 224–25.
[104] Johnson, "Paul and 'The Israel of God': An Exegetical and Eschatological Case-Study'," 187.
[105] Professor David Flusser's "PHARISEES, SADDUCEES AND ESSENES IN PESHER NAHUM" Summary by Harry Gaylord. Page 40. See also: Flusser, Scrolls from the Judean Desert and the Essenes, p. 78
[106] According to the authoritative BDAG / 'Bauer-Danker' Lexicon, "Proton" can either mean first sequentially or in prominence.
[107] The White House, archive, "Remarks by the President in Days of Remembrance Observance." April 24, 2001.
[108] Gerhart Ladner, "Aspects of Patristic Anti-Judaism," *Viator: Medieval and Renaissance Studies* 2 (1971), 362.
[109] Augustine, *Adversus Judaeos* 7, 10, see also 8, 11. "*Occidistis Christum in parentibus vestris.*"
[110] Jerome, *The Homilies of Saint Jerome* (Washington, DC 1964), 1:255, 258–62.
[111] John Chrysostom, *Homilies against Judaizing Christians*, 6.2.10.
[112] *Contra Judaeos*, 1, 18, in Rosemary Ruether, *Faith and Fratricide* (New York 1965), 130.
[113] Quoted by James Parkes, *The Conflict of Church and Synagogue* (New York 1979), 290.
[114] "On the Sabbath," 4:23, in Ruether, *Faith and Fratricide*, 148.
[115] Mary Stroll, *The Jewish Pope: Ideology and Politics in the Papal Schism of 1130* (Leiden 1987), 166.
[116] Quoted in David Kertzer, *The Popes against the Jews: The Vatican's Role in the Rise of Modern Anti-Semitism* (New York 2001), 136–8.
[117] Kertzer, *The Popes against the Jews*, 208.
[118] Kertzer, *The Popes against the Jews*, 210–11.
[119] Charles Glock and Rodney Stark, *Christian Beliefs and Antisemitism* (New York 1966), xvi, 185–7, 50–65, 73–4, 105. See also Rodney Stark et al., *Wayward Shepherds* (New York 1971), 5, 9–10, 50; Alphons Silbermann, *Sind Wir Antisemiten?* (Cologne 1982), 51–2.
[120] Frank Felsenstein, *Antisemitic Stereotypes: A Paradigm of Otherness in English Popular Culture, 1660–1830* (Baltimore 1995); Quillard, *Le Monument Henry*.
[121] Jakob and Wilhelm Grimm, *Deutsches Wörterbuch*, 2nd ed. (Leipzig 1877), Vol. 4, S. 2353.
[122] Célia Szniter Mentlik, "HISTÓRIA, LINGUAGEM E PRECONCEITO: ressonâncias do período inquisitorial sobre o mundo contemporâneo," *Revista História Hoje* 2 (5) (November 2004); http://www.anpuh.uepg.br/ historia-hoje/vo12n5/celia.htm
[123] *Oxford English Dictionary* (Oxford 1933, 1961), 5:576–7; and the *Oxford English Dictionary Supplement* (Oxford 1976), 2:18–19.
[124] See, for example, Fischer, *The History of an Obsession*.
[125] Kertzer, *Popes against the Jews*, 206.
[126] Karl Jaspers, *The Question of German Guilt* (New York 1947), 32.
[127] www.religioustolerance.org/jud_pers1.html John G. Gager, *The Origins of Anti-Semitism* (London: Oxford University Press, 1983), pp. 127-129.
[128] Centre for the Study of Historical Christian Antisemitism, "Justin Martyr," www.hcacentre.org/JustinMartyr.html
[129] LeadershipU, "The Jews as the Christians Saw Them," www.leaderu.com/ftissues/ft9705/articles/wilken. html
[130] Centre for the Study of Historical Christian Antisemitism, "Origen," www.hcacentre.org/Origen.html
[131] California State University at Northridge, "Canons of the Church Council at Elvira (Granada) ca. 309 AD," www.csun.edu/~hcfll004/elvira.html
[132] Centre for the Study of Historical Christian Antisemitism, "John Chrysostom,"

www.hcacentre.org/JohnChrysostom.html
[133] https://www.khouse.org/articles/2020/1372/
[134] Gabriel Wilensky, Six Million Crucifixions: How Christian Teachings About Jews Paved the Road to the Holocaust, (San Diego,CA: QWERTY Publishers, 2010), p. 98.
[135] Ibid., "St. Jerome," www.hcacentre.org/Jerome.html
[136] Ibid., "Saint Augustine," www.hcacentre.org/Augustine.html
[137] John Weiss, *Ideology of Death: Why the Holocaust Happened in Germany*, (Chicago: Ivan R. Dee, 1996) p. 15.
[138] New Advent, "Easter Controversy," www.newadvent.org/cathen/05228a.htm
[139] Bagatti Bellarmino, *The Church from the Circumcision: History and Archaeology of the Judeo-Christians* (Jerusalem: Franciscan Printing Press, 1971), 93.
[140] Gene Shaparenko, The Resurgence of 'Christian' Anti-Semitism," www.aquatechnology.net/RESURGENCE.html
[141] Dr. Louis Goldberg, *God, Torah, Messiah* (San Francisco: Purple Pomegranate Productions, 2009), 128.
[142] *Vita Constantine 3.18,* http://www.newadvent.org/fathers/25023.html.
[143] https://www.chabad.org/library/article_cdo/aid/2617027/jewish/Overview-of-Christian-Antisemitism.html.
[144] G. Sujin, "The Protestant Reformers and the Jews: Excavating Contexts, Unearthing Logic," ed. Christopher Metress, MDPI, Multidisciplinary Digital Publishing Institute, April 20, 2017, www.mdpi.com/2077-1444/8/4/72/html.
[145] Isidore of Seville (1970). Guido Donini (ed.). History of the Goths, Vandals, and Suevi (2 ed.). Leiden: E.J.Brill. pp. 27–28.
[146] Gibb, H. A. R. *The Damascus Chronicle of the Crusades: Extracted and Translated from the Chronicle of Ibn Al-Qalanisi.* Dover Publications, 2003, p. 48
[147] H. A. R. Gibb, *The Damascus Chronicle of the Crusades: Extracted and Translated from the Chronicle of Ibn Al Qalanisi* (Dover Publications, 2003) (ISBN 0486425193).
[148] Remember.org., "Classical and Christian Anti-Semitism," www.remember.org/History.root.classical.html
[149] https://encyclopedia.ushmm.org/content/en/article/blood-libel
[150] Weakland, John (1976). "Pastorelli, Pope, and Persecution: A Tragic Episode in 1320". *Jewish Social Studies.* 38: 1.
[151] Jewish History Sourcebook, "The Expulsion from Spain, 1492 CE," www.fordham.edu/halsall/jewish/1492-jews-spain1.html
[152] See Yosef Yerushalmi, *Assimilation and Racial Antisemitism* (New York 1982); Léon Poliakov, *The Aryan Myth* (New York 1974).
[153] Poliakov, *The Aryan Myth*, 12–13; Albert Sicroff, *Les controverses des statuts de "pureté de sang" en Espange du XVe au XVIIe siècle* (Paris 1960); and Michael Glatzer, "Pablo de Santa Maria on the Events of 1391," in Shmuel Almog, ed., *Antisemitism through the Ages* (Oxford 1988), 127–37.
[154] Cecil Roth, *A History of the Marranos* (New York 1974), 21, 29–30.
[155] Yerushalmi, *Assimilation and Racial Antisemitism*, 10.
[156] Yerushalmi, *Assimilation and Racial Antisemitism*, 9.
[157] Pedro Aznar Cardona, Expulsión Justificada de los Moriscos Españoles, 127-28
[158] Sandoval, *Historia de la vida y hechos del emperator Carlos V*, quoted by Jerome Friedman, "Jewish Conversion, the Spanish Pure Blood Laws and Reformation: A Revisionist View of Racial and Religious Anti-Semitism" (*Sixteenth-Century Journal*), 18 (1) (1987), 16–17.
[159] Vincente da Costa Mattos, *Breve discurso contra a heretica perfidia do judaismo*, quoted by Friedman, "Jewish Conversion, the Spanish Pure Blood Laws and Reformation."
[160] Torrejoncillo, Centinela contra Judios puesta en la torre de la iglesia de Dios (published in 1673, expanded in 1736). See Frank Manuel, Broken Shaft (Cambridge, MA 1992), 223-4, and Yerushalmi, Assimilation and Racial
Antisemitism, 16.
[161] ibid.
[162] James Reites, S.J., "St. Ignatius of Loyola and the Jews," *Studies in the Spirituality of Jesuits* (September 1981), 15, 16, 32.
[163] Reites, "St. Ignatius of Loyola and the Jews."

[164] Peter Godman, *Hitler and the Vatican* (New York 2004), 62.
[165] Shlomo Simonsohn, *The Apostolic See and the Jews: Documents, 1464–1521* (Toronto 1990), docs. 879, 1157, 1158, 1167, 1206, 1334 (hereafter cited as Simonsohn I, II, III); and Shlomo Simonsohn, *The Apostolic See and the Jews: History* (Toronto 1991), 385, 387–91 (hereafter cited as Simonsohn, *History*).
[166] Simonsohn III, docs. 1167 and 1206.
[167] Owen Chadwick, *The Popes and European Revolution* (Oxford 1981), 133.
[168] The Jewish Virtual Library, "Martin Luther: The Jews and Their Lies (1543)," www.jewishvirtuallibrary.org/jsource/anti-semitism/Luther_on_Jews.html
[169] To Pirkheimer and Reuchlin in November 1517. See Heinrich Graetz, *The History of the Jews* (Philadelphia 1940), 4:435, 443–4; Simonsohn, *History*, 333 n101; Heiko Oberman, *The Roots of Antisemitism in the Age of Renaissance and Reformation* (Philadelphia 1981), 30–1, 53.
[170] Quoted by Léon Poliakov, *The History of Antisemitism* (New York 1974), 1:215.
[171] Quoted by Sander Gilman, "Martin Luther and the Self-Hating Jews," in Gerhard Dünnhaupt, ed., *The Martin Luther Quincentennial* (Detroit 1985), 84–8.
[172] Martin Luther, "On the Jews and Their Lies," in *Luther's Works*, trans. Franklin Sherman (Philadelphia 1971), 137–8 (this translation of "Von den Juden und Ihren Lügen," Weimar Edition, 53:417–52, will hereafter be abbreviated as "Jews").
[173] Martin Luther, "That Jesus Christ Was Born a Jew," in Walther Brandt, ed., *Luther's Works* (Philadelphia 1967), 45:213; repeated in *Vom Schem Hamphoras*.
[174] Reinhold Lewin, *Luthers Stellung zu den Juden: Ein Betrag zur Geschichte der Juden während des Reformationszeitalters* (Berlin 1911), 77.
[175] Luther, "Jews," 170, 216–17, 253, 267–9, 285–6. See also Gerhard Falk, *The Jew in Christian Theology* (London 1992), 166–7.
[176] Phyllis Petty, "Christian Hatred and Persecution of the Jews," www.therefinersfire.org/antisemitism_in_church.htm.
[177] Martin Luther, "On the Jews and Their Lies," in LW 47:138-39. See also WA 53:418.
[178] Martin Luther, On the Jews and Their Lies, 1543. Martin H. Bertram, translator, Luther's Works (Philadelphia: Fortress Press, 1971).
[179] Phyllis Petty, "Christian Hatred and Persecution of the Jews," www.therefinersfire.org/antisemitism_in_church.htm, accessed on May 28, 2007.
[180] Ibid
[181] Knox Theological Seminary, "An Open Letter to Evangelicals and Other Interested Parties: The People of God, the Land of Israel, and the Impartiality of the Gospel."
[182] "Ad Quaelstiones et Objecta Juaei Cuiusdam Responsio," by John Calvin; The Jew in Christian Theology, Gerhard Falk, McFarland and Company, Inc., Jefferson, NC and London, 1931.
[183] Ivar Fjeld, The Jewish Martyrs of Old Goa, Golden Heart Emporium Books, 2014, Page 8.
[184] Richard Harries. After the evil: Christianity and Judaism in the shadow of the Holocaust. Oxford University Press, 2003.
[185] Spanish philosopher George Santayana and British statesman Winston Churchill are credited with the aphorism
[186] Martin Luther, "Heidelberg Disputation," Article 21, in *Luther's Works*, 31:40.
[187] Jacob Neusner, "Christian Missionaries—Jewish Scholars," *Midstream* (October 1991), 31.
[188] Hans Küng. On Being a Christian. Doubleday, Garden City NY, 1976
[189] Cited in Richard Steigmann-Gall, *The Holy Reich: Nazi Conceptions of Christianity, 1919–1945* (Cambridge 2003), 1, 4.
[190] Peter Hayes, ed., *Lessons and Legacies* (Evanston 1991), 8.
[191] Raul Hilberg, *The Destruction of the European Jews* (Chicago 1967), 5–7.
[192] See Joshua Trachtenberg, *The Devil and the Jews* (Philadelphia 1961).
[193] See Pierre Quillard, *Le Monument Henry* (Paris 1899); also Stephen Wilson, "Le Monument Henry: La structure de l'antisémtisme en France, 1898–1899," *Annales* 32 (1977).
[194] Steigmann-Gall, *The Holy Reich*, 112. The only paganist to reject Christ was General Ludendorff, and he was the only paganist expelled from the Nazi Party.
[195] Steigmann-Gall, *The Holy Reich*, 3; summarized, 10–12.
[196] Ibid.

[197] *Mythus des 20. Jahrhunderts* (Munich 1930), 391.
[198] See Klaus Fischer, *The History of an Obsession: German Judaeophobia and the Holocaust* (New York 1998).
[199] Robert Alter, "From Myth to Murder," *The New Republic* (20 May 1991), 34, 37–8; Walter Sokel, "Dualistic Thinking and the Rise of Ontological Antisemitism in 19th-Century Germany," in Sander Gilman and Steven Katz, eds., *Antisemitism in Times of Crisis* (New York 1991), 154–72.
[200] Quoted in Bernard Wasserstein, *Britain and the Jews of Europe, 1939–1945* (London 1979), 47.
[201] https://www.theguardian.com/world/2020/sep/16/holocaust-us-adults-study
[202] Ibid.
[203] Jeremy Noakes and Geoffrey Pridham, eds., Nazism 1919-1945, Vol. 1, The Rise to Power 1919-1934. Exeter: University of Exeter Press, 1998, pp. 14-16.
[204] Michalczyk, John J.; Bryant, Michael S.; Michalczyk, Susan A. (10 February 2022). Hitler's 'Mein Kampf' and the Holocaust: A Prelude to Genocide. Also: Rossol, Nadine; Ziemann, Benjamin (6 January 2022). The Oxford Handbook of the Weimar Republic.
[205] Phyllis Petty, "Christian Hatred and Persecution of the Jews."
[206] Akten deutscher Bischöfe, vol. 1, pp. 100-102. Quoted in Saul Friedländer, Nazi Germany and the Jews, p. 47.
[207] John Paul II, "We Remember - Reflection on the Holocaust"
[208] The Washington Post, "Pope Asks Pardon For Sins Of Church", March 13, 2000.
[209] Pope Benedict XVI, "Jesus of Nazareth."
[210] https://www.pbs.org/newshour/show/rise-of-antisemitism-elevates-fears-in-france.
[211] https://www.timesofisrael.com/france-reports-27-increase-in-anti-semitic-acts/.
[212] https://www.adl.org/resources/press-release/us-antisemitic-incidents-hit-highest-level-ever-recorded-adl-audit-finds
[213] https://www.washingtonpost.com/religion/2019/05/01/alleged-synagogue-shooter-was-churchgoer-who-articulated-christian-theology-prompting-tough-questions-evangelical-pastors/.
[214] https://www.nytimes.com/2018/10/28/us/gab-robert-bowers-pittsburgh-synagogue-shootings.html.
[215] www.knoxseminary.org/Prospective/Faculty/WittenbergDoor/index.html
[216] Ibid., section IX
[217] Ibid., conclusion.
[218] John Piper, "Israel, Palestine, and the Middle East, "DesiringGod.org sermon March, 7, 2004
[219] https://www.creativecommunityforpeace.com/about-bds/
[220] https://www.ngo-monitor.org/press-releases/presbyterian-church-officials-promote-bds
[221] https://www.jpost.com/opinion/bds-and-antisemitism-604286
[222] https://www.gov.il/BlobFolder/generalpage/behind_the_mask/en/strategic_affairs_Behind%20The%20MAsk_en.pdf
[223] https://www.ajc.org/news/bds-is-antisemitic
[224] https://growjo.com/company/Christians_United_For_Israel-_CUFI
[225] San Antonio Fundamentalist Battles Anti-Semitism," *Houston Chronicle*, April 30, 1988, sec. 6, pg. 1.
[226] https://www.jpost.com/israel-news/state-of-child-report-finds-1-in-3-children-under-poverty-line-in-israel-520048
[227] https://www.haaretz.com/2013-10-19/ty-article/israel-turns-into-cocaine-trade-hub/0000017f-f4a8-d487-abff-f7fe24850000
[228] https://www.israelhayom.com/2021/04/11/covid-leads-to-12-increase-in-domestic-violence-in-2020-police-reveals/
[229] Israel Central Bureau of Statistics. 29 December 2022. Retrieved 29 December 2022.
[230] Population of Israel on the Eve of 2023 (Report). Israel Central Bureau of Statistics. 29 December 2022.
[231] Christmas 2022 - Christians in Israel". *www.cbs.gov.il*
[232] Miller, Duane Alexander (April 2014). "Freedom of Religion in Israel-Palestine: May Muslims Become Christians, and Do Christians Have the Freedom to Welcome Such Converts?". St Francis Magazine. 10 (1): 17–24.

[233] https://www.theatlantic.com/international/archive/2012/11/kosher-jesus-messianic-jews-in-the-holy-land/265670/
[234] https://www.jpost.com/christianworld/article-696980
[235] https://www.caspari.com/2022/02/07/the-caspari-center-survey-released-the-israeli-messianic-movement-has-more-than-tripled-in-the-last-20-years
[236] "Ray Comfort Was Almost Killed Preaching in Jerusalem." YouTube, Aug 6, 2022.
[237] "Ray Comfort Was Almost Killed Preaching in Jerusalem." YouTube, Aug 6, 2022.
[238] "Genesis 109. Sin's Temporary Consequences." Dr. Andy Woods. Feb 12th, 2023.
[239] שמחה שבל, ספרות המקרא: מבואות ומחקרים - כרך ראשון, ירושלים, בהוצאת: יד יצחק בן-צבי, 2011, עמ' 227- 232
[240] Duignan, Brian, ed. Medieval Philosophy: From 500 CE to 1500 CE. Britannica Educational Publishing, 2010. See also: Stuckey, Tom. The Wrath of God Satisfied?: Atonement in an Age of Violence. Wipf and Stock Publishers, 2012.
[241] https://www.encyclopedia.com/environment/encyclopedias-almanacs-transcripts-and-maps/evangelical-and-fundamental-christianity
[242] https://www.youtube.com/watch?v=aqAuvdEtbCk
[243] "God Hates the Sin and the Sinner - Tim Conway", YouTube, Sep 18, 2018.
[244] Does God Hate People? WyattGraham.com, April 18, 2020.
[245] https://realfaith.com/what-christians-believe/jesus-propitiation-substitute-sins
[246] David Platt, Sep 24, 2011 speech, Desiring God 2011 National Conference.
[247] John MacArthur, "Who Really Killed Jesus?" (gty.org, April 17, 2005). Also in "Who Killed Jesus?, (gty.org, July 10, 2009), MacArthur blamed mankind for killing Jesus, but blaming both makes it sound as if mankind were nothing but a puppet in the hands of God.
[248] David G. Shackelford, "Isaiah 53. Compassion of the Cross" (faithlife.com)
[249] Voddie Baucham, in "American Gospel: Christ Crucified", minute 41.
[250] "Voddie Baucham: Brokenness". YouTube, Aug 11, 2013.
[251] C.J. Mahaney, "The Cross: A Meditation on Jesus' Atoning Death." May 29, 2006. New Attitude Conference; Louisville, KY. Available at https://vimeo.com/5289815, at minute 48.
[252] Paul Washer - Gethsemane
[253] The 2nd of "The Four Spiritual laws."
[254] David Platt, "Radical: Taking Back Your Faith from the American Dream." Multnomah, 2010, pp 35-36.
255 Philip Graham Ryken, "The Heart of the Cross". Crossway, a publishing ministry of Good News Publishers, Wheaton, 2005. Pg 87.
[256] Paul Washer, "Discovering the Glorious Gospel". HeartCry Missionary Society, Third edition; 2021, pp 49.
[257] My emphasis in bold; "What are the consequences of sin?", GotQuestion website.
[258] Francis Chan, "Crazy Love", page 201.
[259] Does God Hate People? WyattGraham.com, April 18, 2020.
[260] David Platt, Sep 24, 2011 speech, Desiring God 2011 National Conference.
[261] Mark Driscoll, "Jesus Sweats Blood", realfaith.com
[262] John MacArthur, "Sin Didn't Kill Jesus, God Did," Crossway, 28 March 2018.
[263] John MacArthur, "Who Killed Jesus?" Grace to You, 10 July 2009.
[264] John Piper, The Pleasure of God in Bruising the Son, March 8, 1987.
[265] John Piper, The Passion of Jesus Christ (Wheaton: Crossway, 2004), 11. For a helpful response to Piper, see Zach Hoag, "3 Reasons God Did Not Kill Jesus (But Jesus Still Had to Die," http://zhoag.com/3-reasons-god-did-not-kill-jesus-but-jesus-still-had-to-die/.
[266] Wayne Grudem, Systematic Theology: An Introduction to Biblical Doctrine (Grand Rapids: Zondervan, 1994), page 574.
[267] Dan Wallace, Professor of Greek at Dallas Theological Seminary: "An Excruciating Gift - Daniel B. Wallace", YouTube, Feb 19, 2019.
[268] Trevin Wax, "Who Killed Jesus?" The Gospel Coalition Blog. 20 March 2007.

[269] Paul Washer, The Gospel's Power and Message (page 192, 194)
[270] "Love and Anger at the Cross?" Nick Batzig, January 6, 2019. Reformation21.org
[271] Living Better 50 Magazine, April 14, 2021 devotional.
[272] https://realfaith.com/what-christians-believe/jesus-propitiation-substitute-sins
[273] C.J. Mahaney, "The Cross: A Meditation on Jesus' Atoning Death." May 29, 2006. New Attitude Conference; Louisville, KY. Available at https://vimeo.com/5289815, at minute 48.
[274] "Animal Sacrifice? Really?", bibleproject.com
[275] "Tom Wright's Cross Centred Revolution," Premier Christianity, February 2017. See also N. T. Wright, The Day the Revolution Began: Reconsidering the Meaning of Jesus's Crucifixion (New York: HarperCollins, 2016).
[276] https://faithgateway.com/blogs/christian-books/no-merit-of-my-own-righteousness
277 David Platt, "God hates Sinners, not just the sin - David Platt" YouTube, Jan 25, 2013.
[278] K. R. Hendren, "Haish Hahu", Keren Or books. Tel-Aviv, 1987, page 96. Translated from Hebrew.
[279] R.C. Sproul, https://www.youtube.com/watch?v=aqAuvdEtbCk
[280] John Piper, "God Loves the Sinner, But Hates the Sin?", July 30, 2013.
[281] Mark Driscoll, "Jesus Sweats Blood", realfaith.com
[282] David Platt, "What Did Jesus Really Mean When He Said Follow Me?", page 8.
[283] Mitchell Dahood S.J., Psalms I: 1-50: Introduction, Translation, and Notes, vol. 16, Anchor Yale Bible (New Haven; London: Yale University Press, 2008), 31.
[284] Willem A. VanGemeren, "Psalms," in The Expositor's Bible Commentary: Psalms, Proverbs, Ecclesiastes, Song of Songs, ed. Frank E. Gaebelein, vol. 5 (Grand Rapids, MI: Zondervan Publishing House, 1991), 88.
[285] Jeff A. Benner, The Ancient Hebrew Lexicon of the Bible, Virtual bookworm, 2005.

Printed in Great Britain
by Amazon